WAR AT SEA

WAR AT SEA

Edward Smithies
with
Colin John Bruce

Constable · London

First published in Great Britain 1992
by Constable and Company Limited
3 The Lanchesters, 162 Fulham Palace Road, London W6 9ER

Copyright © 1992 by Edward Smithies and Colin John Bruce

ISBN 0 09 471590 4

The right of Edward Smithies and Colin John Bruce to be
identified as the authors of this work has been asserted by them
in accordance with the Copyright, Designs and Patents Act 1988
Set in 11pt Linotype Sabon
by Servis Filmsetting Ltd, Manchester
Printed in Great Britain
by
St Edmundsbury Press Ltd
Bury St Edmunds, Suffolk
A CIP catalogue record for this book
is available from the British Library

For Edward

CONTENTS

List of illustrations · ix

Acknowledgements · xi

1   Introduction · 1

2   The Regulars · 15

3   Merchant Service · 59

4   Dockyard Hands · 80

5   Wavy Navy · 85

6   Hostilities Only · 103

7   Soldiers at Sea · 141

8   Fleet Air Arm · 150

9   Submariners · 166

10   Bootnecks · 175

11   WRNS · 184

12   Survivors · 191

List of Illustrations

between pages 116 and 117

Designed during the First World War and lost during the
Second. The graceful battlecruiser HMS *Hood*
Boiler room of a battleship
Destroyer deck in heavy weather
Lookout on board HMS *Suffolk* surveys the ice floes of the
Denmark Strait
Spectacular explosion of the US ammunition ship *Mary
Luckenbach*, taken from the flight deck of the escort
carrier HMS *Avenger*
Replacing the losses. A cargo ship and tanker in the fitting
out basin
Dockyard matey at work on the screw of a cruiser
Shell room of a destroyer. Loading up the hoist with four
more rounds
Double-decker bus converted for use in training Merchant
Navy gunners
Packed hangar deck of a carrier
'Batsman' and Swordfish during a deck landing
Control room of a submarine
Wrens at the rifle range, with a Royal Marines instructor
Carrier HMS *Ark Royal* capsizing off Gibraltar, after being
torpedoed by the U-81

All illustrations are reproduced by kind permission
of The Imperial War Musuem, London

Acknowledgements

This book was compiled from a selection of the conversations and correspondence Edward conducted with people kind enough to share their memories with him. Where requested, I have used pseudonyms in the text. There is not space to acknowledge everyone who gave their time, but I would like to thank the following without whom this book could not have been written:

Mr D. Adams, Mrs A.D. Allsop, Messrs R. Barclay, L. Beavan, R. Bennett, H. Bird, W. Brettingham, A. Burke and A. Burns, Miss E. Catt, Messrs C.F. Corpes, C.F.J.L. Davies, R. Farrell, A. Francis, K. Goose, F. Graham, J. Green and S. Hall, Miss P. Hansell, Mr F. Hardy, Mrs E. Harrison, Mr and Mrs Hibbert, Messrs F. Holliday, E. Johnson, J.R. Kelleher, W. Kellie, K.C. Kimber, A. Lines, L. Mason, S. Mayes, R.R. Meade and D. Merrin, Miss M. Moxley, Messrs W. Mutimer, J. Parren Agate, S. Philps, A. Pizer, R. Pridham-Wippel, H. Richardson, K. Roberts, L. Roberts, A. Rose, W. Sarginson, G. Sear and W.E. See, Mr and Mrs Sergeant, Mrs E. Shaw, Messrs R. Shepherd, W. Smith, H. Spensley, E. Thomas, G. Thomas, R.R. Thuillier, H. Trace, E. Tubb, H. Usher, J. Wall, G. Ward, A. Wilson, C. Wines, F. Wright and G. Wright.

1

INTRODUCTION

The untimely death of Edward Smithies in 1991 deprived oral history of one of its most enthusiastic and skilful exponents.

His *War in the Air*, published to critical acclaim in 1990, had explored the RAF's war – the way it impinged on the lives of the ordinary people caught up in the great campaigns of 1939–45, be they service personnel or civilians – in a way which brought home the events of those years at a human level. *War at Sea*, research for which had begun while its predecessor was in preparation, was intended to extend the same coverage to the various Naval services, whose achievements have often in the past been overlooked despite their crucial contribution to the Allied victory.

Sadly this was not a project he was to see completed, and the task of writing a book based on his vast correspondence and the transcripts of his many interviews thus fell to me.

Unlike Edward, who had spent his formative years surrounded by the sights and sounds of the wartime aircraft industry (in which his father worked), I was born too late to have any direct experience of the war – my parents were still in their teens when it ended. I was raised in Elgin, a county town in the rich farmlands which stretch along the coast of the Moray Firth between the mountains and the sea.

The area had a strong maritime heritage because of the fishing industry and, when I was a child, a highly visible Royal Navy presence in the form of a Royal Naval Air Station at Lossiemouth, five miles from my home.

Open days at the base were a treat I always eagerly awaited. Looking back, the effort put into making these a success seems to have been a good investment, as the Navy's time at Lossie (the base was handed back to the RAF in 1972) are universally viewed with nostalgia by the locals.

These visits were my first brush with the Navy as an institution. Even at that tender age I found it extraordinary that every possible measure seemed to be taken to suspend reality and preserve the illusion of the base actually being a ship. It had a ship's name – HMS *Fulmar* – and flew the White Ensign at the mast. It had a wardroom for the officers, a quarterdeck, Chief Petty Officers' and Petty Officers' messes. Anyone on the base was referred to as being 'on board', and anyone off the base as 'ashore'.

Though I did not recognize it at the time, this was typical of the Navy's boundless self-confidence, the reasons for which were not hard to find.

In 1939 the Royal Navy was the force which bound the Empire together, kept the home islands safe from foreign invasion and enabled the huge British merchant fleet to cruise the world's oceans without interference. New entrants were always made to feel that they were the heirs to a proud tradition, and that to tarnish that image through their own actions would be unforgivable. Inevitably this made it conservative in outlook, and deeply suspicious of new ideas. But the very nature of its all-enveloping control over the life of the individual appealed to many who signed on. The sense of belonging to a service with an unbroken history of success stretching back to the previous century was a very powerful one.

Since time immemorial we had had the greatest Navy in the world. It was a national institution. It was the senior service – legendary, beloved of everyone. Jolly Jack was tremendously popular ashore, and there were sailors to be seen everywhere. There were superstitions like touching a sailor's collar for luck. Abroad, honorary membership of clubs to officers of visiting ships was automatic. Cheques could be cashed virtually anywhere without question. 'Gangway for a Naval Officer was very much the order of the day. (*Mr Roberts*)

The Royal Navy's peacetime duties largely revolved around 'showing the flag' – in other words maintaining a presence in foreign waters to keep an eye on British interests. The entire globe was divided into patrol areas, known as stations, to which ships were periodically rotated. The most sought-after of these were the America and West Indies Station, covering the Caribbean, the west and east coasts of the USA and the west coast of South America; and the China Station, which covered most of the Far East, including Hong Kong and Shanghai.

Shanghai was a place that we all looked forward to – it was the best place in the Far East. Probably the least interesting was Hong Kong, which was nice, but again it was very exclusive. We were restricted to the Wanchai area. You'd get entertainment there, and they had a sailors' club with billiard tables – I was a very keen snooker player.

Our base was at Hong Kong, but in fact we spent most of the time at Wei-hai-wei. It was our sports field, our summer home. You were either there or on cruises, or in wintertime you went down to Hong Kong. Shanghai was purely a visiting port. We went there two or three times – I always thought of it as a very civilized place. It was sophisticated. There were a lot of foreigners, the place was absolutely full of them. We would tie up opposite the Bund and meet other ships, from other navies; perhaps an American or Dutch ship would be in there and you would exchange courtesy visits – even the lower grades; the stokers would go and see a film on the American ship or they'd come and see a film on yours. (*Mr Farrell*)

Pre-war commissions were for two to two and a half years, with no opportunity for home leave until the ship returned to her base in the UK. Usually these cruises were a matter of routine, but occasionally they could be enlivened by some unexpected action.

We had newly commissioned the *Ajax* in Portsmouth – though we were a Chatham crew – and had recently arrived in Bermuda to work up to full fighting efficiency, when we received orders to proceed at full speed to Kingston, Jamaica to 'put down riots' on the banana plantations!

Off we went, and during the passage our landing organization was perfected and we were exercised in street-fighting techniques.

As soon as we had anchored, shore patrols were landed to back up the local police force, and were based in the main police station. The next day we were recalled on board and the *Ajax* sailed to show ourselves to the plantations and advertise our presence. As we slowly steamed round the coast they could see us from all the estates up on the hills. This stratagem appeared to work, for when we returned to anchor in Kingston harbour we found that the emergency was now over. Having had a very hectic three or four days we were given a 'make and mend' – that is, a half day's holiday – and we all very promptly got our heads down.

Before long the loudspeakers called us to fall in, much to our annoyance. There was a lot of grumble, grumble, grumble! The Commander addressed us: His Excellency Sir Edward Denham, Governor of Jamaica, has just died. It is our duty, as the senior service present on the island, to organize and carry out a State Funeral tomorrow.' So goodbye 'make and mend'.

Soon we had seamen platoons organized for numerous public duties, and funeral drills were being rehearsed. The rest of the afternoon and dog watches were spent in ironing No.1 suits and collars, cleaning boots and equipment, and preparing for the varied duties that had been allotted to us.

Next morning an officer and a small group of four Leading Seamen – I was one – and two Royal Marines Corporals, with our rifles and bayonets, found ourselves in Kingston Parish Church at 7.30 a.m. The late Governor, in his coffin, was already there in the chancel. The official lying-in-state was to commence at 8 a.m., when the public would be permitted to enter.

Two Leading Seamen, one Corporal of the Royal Marines and one Corporal of the Sherwood Foresters – the local garrison – were to stand at each corner of the catafalque, rigidly in the resting on the arms reversed position, with head bowed over the rifle butt so we could see nothing except the floor at our feet.

The doors opened, the public streamed in and shuffled past the catafalque in continuous single file until the doors were finally closed at 4 p.m. We guards were relieved every fifteen minutes, when we had a glass of lemonade and a seat in the vestry.

It was quite fascinating to watch the feet as they filed by. Many were white, but quite a number were black. Many were well shod, some very poorly shod, some were bare-footed. I passed the time speculating as to their nationality and social position – beggars, fishermen, children, solicitors, labourers, clerks, soldiers – the procession was endless, all day. When the doors finally closed we guards were told we were to escort the hearse, four on each side, as the cortège made its progress through the streets of Kingston down to the dockside.

The procession, consisting of detachments of the Royal Navy, the Royal Marines, the Sherwood Foresters, the Jamaican Police, the Town Council and many other civic groups – with four bands – made its way through crowded streets, we guards marching with arms reversed. Arriving at the quayside the coffin went aboard *Ajax* and was placed on its own in the centre of the quarterdeck.

As soon as we were all aboard, we proceeded slowly down the bay with Ensigns at half mast. We eventually hove to about three miles off Plum Point. There – at about 6 p.m. just as the sun was sinking into the western sea – the coffin was consigned to the ocean together with many wreaths. The Ensigns were hoisted right up, the ship gathered speed and we left the wreaths floating in a calm sea. (*Mr Parren Agate*)

Behind the Navy, supplying it with the ships and equipment it needed, was a vast shipbuilding and armaments industry.

In West Hartlepool, it was the steelworks, the shipyard or the pits. Amazing it was to go through the steelworks – to see the ingots come down . . . and come out as inch plate at the other end of the rolling mills; ship's plating, about twenty, thirty foot long. My eldest brother worked in the pattern shop – that was amongst the woodwork – and he always said to me I was frightened of the steelworks. He was right, I was. Everything was dangerous, they had some terrible accidents. (*Mr Sarginson*)

Brought up in Birkenhead there was little doubt about which service to join. At school, in the Twenties, we were always given a day off for a major launch. The weather was always marvellous. So a saying came into being – when it was sunny 'There must be a launch at Cammell Lairds'! (*Mr Trace*)

But the shipyards, like the aircraft industry, had suffered heavily from post-First World War cutbacks and from the world-wide slump.

The Merchant Navy too found itself chasing fewer and fewer cargoes, with the collapse of British coal exports hitting the tramp operators particularly hard. Millions of tons were laid up, and experienced seamen and officers joined those ships still at sea in menial positions just to find work.

In South Shields there'd be, oh, two hundred men there all waiting for jobs. And every river you looked at, the Tyne, the Tees, the Wear, there'd be ships laid up there at their buoys, rusting. No cargoes. This was in 1932. When I paid off they said don't come back here, there's no work – and there won't be. (*Mr Graham*)

British operating costs were higher than those of most of their foreign competitors, which led to them being squeezed badly as business contracted. It was also a matter of considerable annoyance to British shipowners that while foreign governments – for example the Scandinavians, the Americans and the French – assisted their merchant fleets with state subsidies, their own government refused to do so.

Not until 1935 did the British merchant fleet receive even a meagre helping hand from government, and by that time the worst of the slump was already over.

Only the tanker fleet actually expanded during the interwar period, as the global demand for oil grew. Overall, the proportion of the world's tonnage under the Red Ensign declined from 48 per cent in 1914 to 32.5 per cent in 1937.

Naval Estimates remained miserly throughout the early thirties, against a darkening world background.

In May 1935 Hitler abrogated the Versailles Peace Treaty, and slightly less than a year later occupied and remilitarized the Rhine-land. Also in 1936 Italy left the League of Nations, the Rome-Berlin Axis was made public, Japan stepped up her attempts to subdue China by force, and civil war erupted in Spain, resulting in the need for the Royal Navy to maintain an increased presence in that region.

When war finally came in 1939 the Navy began a huge expansion, with most of the manpower being provided by conscripts. Inevitably training for the new intakes, for which the Navy commandeered holiday camps like the one at Skegness, ran on the 'sausage machine' principle. The military nature of the training also came as a surprise to many.

There was too many. There was hundreds going through Skegness every week; they were just cannon fodder I suppose. They were just getting them through as fast as they could. In a few weeks we were trained, we did rifle drill, we squarebashed – sailors! Going on board a ship! But of course it's the discipline. They didn't care what you were suffering, half past five in the morning, free-ee-zing cold, PT, doing press ups, and you had to do them or you'd get a foot in your back. No pretending. Those weeks I think were the worst – even worse than actual action! (*Mr Ward*)

Another surprise often awaited the new sailor when he discovered what job the Navy wanted him to do. Those destined for the more technical trades frequently found the compressed wartime courses a particular struggle.

A four year course before the war was condensed into six months. I was an electrician on Grumman Hellcats. They were terrors; I didn't like them at all. In our oral test for our exam, a chap would stand there with a handful of nuts and bolts, and he'd tell you to describe a normal hydraulic system. Get half way through and he'd suddenly say 'What size is that bolt?' So you really had to use your brain to learn. I was in a classroom from about seven in the morning till seven at night . . . (*Mr Goose*)

For others, merely adjusting to life afloat was bad enough.

We went out into the open sea, and from nothing it was going up and down about twenty feet. That's no exaggeration at all. We knew what weightlessness was long before they ever tried people on it – you'd walk along the passageway of a destroyer, and your legs . . . You're pawing at air for a moment; you're sliding against the bulkhead on one side, then across to the other, and then you get about ten times your weight, as she comes up again. (*Mr Brettingham*)

We always said they must have designed the ships first with the officers in mind, second with the guns in mind, third with the engines in mind, and finally where the hell are we going to put the crew? And they found little places to put the crew in [laughs]. This is the way it seemed. When you're trying to get through a flat, hammocks swinging about, and it's always damp because of the metal, always condensation. Nobody liked battleships – it was just like being on shore, the regimentation. Like rig of the day. Rig of the day was always announced, and woe betide anybody who wasn't in the right uniform. As the ships got smaller, so your discipline eased up – you became a very much closer-knit community on a small ship. (*Mr Adams*)

For a large proportion of each crew, their action stations would be a totally enclosed space in the bowels of the ship – often several decks down and offering little opportunity either to follow what was going on or to escape if disaster were to strike.

'Being in the engine room I knew little, and saw less, of the actual war. I heard the bombs and felt them, but we just steamed the ship – and went to the cinema to see the war we had been in the middle of!' (*Mr Bennett*)

On the destroyer my action station was in the after shell room. It comes over the tannoy, 'Action stations', you stop what you're doing, rush aft and go straight down into the shell room. Then the hatch is put down and bolted, so there's no way of getting out. Once you're down there and you're locked in, that becomes a watertight compartment, so if the ship's damaged or anything . . .
You've had it
Exactly. And to give you an instance of that, we were down

there one night, and what you had was a little lift which drops down and takes four shells at a time. They're either armour-piercing, or shrapnel, or star shells, or whatever – if it was star shells you had to fuse the damn things before you put them in; they shout down the voice tube to tell you what setting they want, what height in the sky they want them to explode at. Anyway, the lift came down and the two of us loaded it up. I shouted for them to hoist it; nothing happened. I kept shouting, still nothing. Then after two or three minutes there's a scurry of footsteps, up went the lift, so I shouted up 'Where you bloody lot been, then? I've been shouting for ages to take that up!' He said, 'Well, there was two torpedoes heading for us!' 'Where'd you go?' 'We all ran for'ard'!' So I said 'Well, what about us stuck down here?' 'You had nothing to worry about' he said, 'you wouldn't have known a thing'.

Did you feel like a victim being put down there?

Well, somebody has to go. It was just your job. (*Mr Meade*)

The Navy's pre-war regulars were at first openly dismissive of the wartime conscripts, but some at least came to applaud the strides the newcomers had made.

We had a Captain who was a regular, a First Lieutenant who was a regular but not a very good one, the other officers were all RNVR, and they sent us a crowd of seamen who had never been to sea before – come straight from barracks, called up, six weeks. And I think we had three experienced Able Seamen, and a Coxswain, and I was a Petty Officer. We had to act as an escort for our convoy on the way down, so the Captain some-how got in touch with the Admiralty and they sent half a dozen experienced Able Seamen and a couple more senior rates.

We trained these kids up as much as we could in the Clyde, on gunnery and this sort of thing, then off we went. And we hit the most terrible weather – the liners were taking seas right over the top.

By the time we got to the Cape they were first class. Mind you they were a bit bolshie to start with. But in a matter of a couple of months they were sailors, and good ones too. We had always said before the war it took five years to make a sailor.

When they had to row a sea boat they were all sixes and sevens, that you would expect, but as sailors doing a basic job aboard a ship they were good. (*Mr Rose*)

Very often the sea itself was the greatest enemy, capable of inflicting tremendous punishment in heavy weather. In one famous incident a wave ripped the armoured roof off a gun turret of the cruiser *Sheffield*, and lesser damage was a regular occurrence.

Our main worry most of the time was the terrible weather we experienced when we had to go north up near Iceland, and across and down to Halifax, Nova Scotia – a place I got to know well. On my first convoy to there the weather was especially bad, and the Captain called me up on deck to signal a ship which was falling back on the flank. She had broken radio silence to say that she had been stove in by the heavy seas and was sinking. I tried to contact her without success, and she continued to fall back. She sent another message, but we couldn't help her because if we'd turned to starboard broadside on to the gale we'd have gone over I think. So she was lost through the sea and not through enemy action. (*Mr Johnson*)

Sharing these dangers equally were the men of the Merchant Navy, most of whom served in slow and vulnerable ships – often with explosive or inflammable cargoes.

When I was on a tanker, I told people that I couldn't swim, so although they might stand some chance if we were torpedoed, I wouldn't be able to help myself if blown into the water. They looked at me in amazement, and one said 'We're carrying high octane petrol. If we get hit it won't *matter* who can swim – we'll all be blown to smithereens'. (*Mr Philps*)

On my first trip to sea on the MV *Port Montreal*, when I was sixteen, our ship was torpedoed at daybreak. After swimming in the sea amongst the wreckage I managed to find a liferaft, and was on it some time before being picked up by a passing lifeboat. What stands out the most vividly is being in the lifeboat and a U-boat bow coming up out of the sea as she surfaced.

We had all heard stories about U-boats machine-gunning survivors, and I think all hands feared the worst and were prepared to go over the side and take their chances. I prayed like I'd never done before.

But the commanding officer hailed us to heave to, and asked us the name of our ship, her tonnage, port of registration, the cargo we were carrying, destination and last port of call. We gave him the information required – we were the *Port Montreal*, outward bound for Australia with a general cargo and a deck cargo of aircraft.

His answer was 'I am sorry – but it is the fortunes of war', and wished us luck. All our crew's eyes were transfixed to the U-boat until the last of its conning tower slipped beneath the waves again. (*Mr Wall*)

The thing was, during the war, we had no uniforms – they gave us these little 'MN' badges, that's all we had, to distinguish us from being a layabout or civilian.

In case people accused you of shirking?

Well they did! People used to come up if you was on a bus – I might be going to join a ship, and they might say 'Look at that bloody bloke down there, what's he doing?' I'd probably just come off an Atlantic run! They didn't know, though. (*Mr Beavan*)

The standard countermeasure against attack, which had proven its worth in the First World War, was to form the merchantmen into tight convoys – where warships could more easily protect them. But the problem was that there were never enough warships to go round.

'You'd have a convoy of sixteen ships, and you'd be lucky if you got two escorts, two corvettes – I'm not talking about anything sophisticated. You felt safe because they were there, though really they were quite ineffective.' (*Mr Smith*)

Convoy assembly procedure was for the ships to sail from port in single file and then form into a large rectangle of, say, ten columns of five or six ships each. A convoy covered a sea area of several square miles. Before leaving port each ship was given a positional number, like 5D – fifth column, fourth ship in that column – and the ship remained in that position for the ocean crossing. Oil tankers and cargo ships carrying vital supplies like steel, munitions, crated aircraft, were positioned in the middle columns with less chance of being sunk by U-boat attacks, though as the war progressed some daring U-boat Captains would submerge in the path of a convoy at night, and as the ships passed over them they'd surface and sink ships in the centre of the convoy from close range. They then crash dived and attempted to escape. (*Mr Mayes*)

Added to the physical dangers for the men at sea were the worries about families back home, who themselves were often under air attack. Separations were lengthy.

MRS HIBBERT: Little Maureen was six months old when he went, and when he came home after two years she was grown. He came home and she fled for her life! He was in his uniform, like. She was really scared, wasn't she?

MR HIBBERT: Yes. That's another funny thing, when you came home – I've seen all these films where they come home and they cuddle each other. Well, I always felt a little bit – you know what I mean?

MRS HIBBERT: With Maureen, I always talked about him and had his picture there, but when they're young and they grow up, it's very difficult.

MR SERGEANT: When I got torpedoed, we weren't married, so my mother had the telegram to say I was missing. And she didn't have anything then till she got a letter from me.

MRS SERGEANT: He was missing for three months.

MR SERGEANT: I wrote a letter from the West Indies, and that was the first they heard that I was alive.

MRS SERGEANT: When you got letters you got about ten at once. They always put numbers on them, so I read them in order. Every time he came back it was like meeting him for the first time. We were married on the Saturday and he went back on the Tuesday, and he was away for eighteen months.

But many women served too, in non-combat capacities. The reborn Women's Royal Naval Service provided many thousands of personnel, who served all over the world.

Perhaps I joined the WRNS because I was born in Milford Haven and whilst most of my parents' family and forefathers had been farmers in that area for hundreds of years, they also had a lot to do with the sea. One of my uncles was a pilot, another an engineer on a fishing boat, and another harbour master at Milford Haven during the war years. But perhaps it just appealed to me – I quite liked the uniform. Apart from one dreadful day when, after shortening the skirt to what I thought was an appropriate length, I appeared on the parade ground to be asked in a loud, clear voice by the officer in charge if I thought I was participating in a ballet! (*Mrs Harrison*)

Being the eldest of a draft of ten, I was put in charge from Mill Hill to Machrihanish. Unfortunately the travel document was therefore headed 'Catt, and nine wrens'. This caused considerable humour among RTOs (*Railway Transport Officers*) en route. (*Miss Catt*)

The war was obviously not without its humour, and even a run ashore sometimes had its own hazards.

We ran two trips to Greece escorting convoys of troopships filled with Australian and New Zealand soldiers. We had met some of them ashore in Alexandria – they were a wild bunch! We had the chance of shore leave whilst berthed in Piraeus, and we were sitting having a quiet beer in a taverna that evening, when a row broke out between the barman and some Aussies. He was refusing to sell them any more beer, saying they'd had enough, and when they disagreed and started to smash the place up, he brought in the MPs, who calmed them down and made them leave. We all carried on with our beers. Ten minutes later the door burst open, a drunken Aussie staggered in, shouted 'Share that, yer Pommie bastards!' and rolled a grenade across the floor between the tables!

Those nearest the door dived out, I got over and behind the bar counter, and we all held our breath waiting for the explosion. Nothing happened. The grenade turned out to be a dummy, a practice one. But a fright like that was enough for one night, so I made my way back to the ship. (*Mr Kellie*)

But underlying everything was the grim reality of being at war.

To me, the war is the most vivid experience of my life, the whole lot. And yet when I talk to youngsters, it's just history to them. It's not history to me. Your whole mentality is different in wartime from what it is in peacetime. You're on the alert the whole time. I wouldn't say you're on edge or anything like that – it's just a different life. (*Mr Thomas*)

I don't think the people at home ever comprehended what it was like. Because they didn't see us as we were, unshaven, unwashed, and looking haggard, twitching a bit. They saw you coming home, you know, buttons, braid. You didn't tell them the whole story because you didn't want to worry them. I don't think they could possibly visualize what the war at sea was like. (*Mr Burke*)

2

THE REGULARS

The regulars of the Royal Navy were all long-service professionals, recruited voluntarily. Seamen signed on for a standard twelve-year term of enlistment, successful completion of which entitled them to the option of signing on for another ten, and to a pension at the end of that time.

Youngsters joining before the age of eighteen, as the Navy was keen to encourage them to do, were rated as Boys. Service as a Boy Seaman did not count towards 'their twelve', this being calculated from their eighteenth birthday, the point at which they officially made the transition to adulthood and were rerated as Ordinary Seamen.

Arthur Rose joined the interwar Navy as a Boy, and was raised in the hard school of the training ships.

I came from a naval family, and I was actually born in Portsmouth, so it was natural that I should go into the Navy. I went through the training ships – HMS *St Vincent* was the one I went to – which I think frankly not enough has been said about, because you've got to remember the Navy was an important part of the nation in those days, and many of the people who went into the Navy did so through these training ships, though there were people who entered at the age of eighteen. Well it wasn't much of a shock to me because at the time I lived practically outside the training establishment, I could hear the bugles going all the time. It was a great shock to a lot of boys, but to me it wasn't. All the same, I must say it was the hardest period of my life.

You went in and you started in what was known as the New Entries Block, where you were segregated from all the other boys for a period of a fortnight. There you were graded into three separate grades, for education, and from that if you were bright enough you went on to a fourth grade which was known as the advanced class grade, and you wore a star on your sleeve. Apart from that you learned to sew, because you had to sew your name and your dormitory number in every item of clothing that you had – that included towels, underwear, flannels, so it was a pretty terrific task. And it all had to be done in a certain way with chain stitching, so many stitches per letter. Each name was examined when you finished it, and you weren't allowed to go ashore – normally you got ashore for half a day after the first three weeks – until you had finished all your sewing to the satisfaction of the Petty Officer instructors.

If you didn't already swim you had to learn, and pass a swimming test which was pretty hectic, fully clothed. The other thing you learned very thoroughly was parade drill, and that was pretty tough. There were no concessions to cold weather or anything like that. If the weather was cold you wore the same clothing as if the weather was warm. And your basic outfit, except on Sundays when you wore a blue sailor suit, was a white 'duck' suit. In the winter period, which I think was from 1st October to 1st May, instead of wearing a flannel under that you wore a jersey, but you never wore an overcoat on the parade ground. The Marines did – you could be standing beside Royal Marines in big overcoats – but sailors never. And no gloves.

Anyway, after three weeks of learning the basics of the Navy – what it's all about, what the ranks and all that sort of thing were, and a bit about the history of the Navy, you moved into what was known as the preliminary class. I think you did three weeks there, where you learned a bit more about the Navy, you went more deeply into seamanship, and you did more parade work. Then you were divided into what were known as parts of ship – there was the forecastle foretop, maintop and quarter-deck – those were the four basic divisions that seamen were allocated to on all the Navy's big ships. There were four large blocks in the training establishment, and each one was a part of ship. First of all I went into the quarterdeck, and then the forecastle after that. Usually you remained in the same one – I only moved because of educational factors. You could be what was known as GC1, which was reckoned to be the top, GC2 or GC3, and you were streamed accordingly. If you were in GC1 you were allowed to sit an advanced class test, and if you passed you became a member of what was known as the advanced class. In each part of ship you had a number of classes – there would always be two running parallel to one another, there would be a general course, or GC, class and an advanced class. Educationally the standards were quite high, particularly if you were in the advanced class, and if you came from an ordinary secondary modern school you were probably taught things you would never have been taught otherwise, such as a bit of advanced electricity. So a boy who emerged from a training ship, if he was of average brightness, was probably better educated than his contemporaries, which is an interesting fact because people always regard servicemen as being a bit dim!

Life in the training ship was very strictly disciplined. You walked nowhere except after five o'clock – you ran everywhere. You got up at, I think, quarter past six in the morning, and the first thing you did was clean ship. You had various parts of the barracks to clean, and if you were unfortunate and you were responsible for the cleaning of the heavy gun battery, or things associated with that, where they had wooden decks, you scrubbed it in bare feet winter and summer. I've seen many boys absolutely crying with pain, because your feet aren't just cold, they're hurting like blazes.

Then you had breakfast, then you went on to instruction, which was either school, seamanship or gunnery. You came back for lunch, then in the winter – there were two routines, winter and summer – you went to sports, which meant dispersing to all the various sports fields round about the town. You came back for tea, then you went to instruction again and then you had supper and went up to your dormitories and polished the floor. Now in summer the routine was the other way round – you went through instruction during the day and you had sport in the evening, including rowing and sailing. We used to have to row these big whalers and enormous cutters up and down Portsmouth harbour.

Once a week you got up at four o'clock in the morning to wash your clothes. You would run across the establishment, which was very big, to the washroom. There, around the walls, were large deep enamel basins, and you ran like mad with your dhobeying [laundry] which was in a pillow slip, in order to get a basin where you did your washing. If you didn't get a basin you had to kneel on the concrete floor and do your dhobeying in a corrugated iron trough there.

Pipe down [lights out] was at nine o'clock at night, and if there was any noise in the dormitory after nine, or if there was any misdemeanour of any kind, the instructor would probably have the whole dormitory out, over the mast, in bare feet, in the dark, winter or summer. You could always tell which class was in trouble because you could hear them going over the mast – and that mast was 150 feet high.

As an indication of the sort of discipline we had, it's worth noting what happened at meal times. You all fell in on the parade ground if it was dry, or in the drill shed if it was wet. The boys detailed as cooks had previously got all the food from the galley and taken it to the messdecks, and as they came to the door and waved a dishcloth to say that the tables were laid, each part of ship was doubled into its own dining hall. You doubled in and you kept quiet, you took your hat off and hung it on a peg, you doubled along to your own mess table and then you stood rigidly to attention behind the stool. When you were all in, the duty instructor blew a whistle, and each boy had to lean forward, pick up his meal – which might be two plates, and try and get a mug as well, and a hunk of bread – and hold it up like that. The instructor would say 'Any boy not got a meal? Any spare meals? Meals down'! when that was done he would blow a whistle again and give the order 'Carry on!', and the routine was you had to put your left foot – not your right foot – over the stool, then right foot over the stool, stand to attention, and then sit down. And no sooner had you started than they'd blow the whistle again to say grace!

That's the sort of discipline. Remember we're talking about the tail end of the Victorian-Edwardian era really. But backing all that was a terrific understanding of boys' problems. They did instill into you a great pride and a great loyalty, so there must have been some good in it

Did boys run away?

Oh yes, occasionally, yes they did. Not all that often. I think during my eighteen or nineteen months in *St Vincent* probably three ran away, and there were fifteen hundred boys. But you see running away was more difficult in those days – where would you go? I've no doubt there would have been more if they could, but then they knew they would be brought back, because you couldn't get out of the Navy!

By the time you finished the training ship you were pretty well imbued with the spirit of the Navy, and you were then anxious to get to sea.

Well, I went to the *Hood* – that was my first ship. I think we had about 250 boys. It was always reckoned that the boys' division was the most efficient part of the ship, because they were so keen. They'd just learned all they had to learn, and they were anxious to have a go at new things. But there was a strict hierarchy on board ship to which the boys were expected to conform, and one of the first things was that they were not allowed to mix with the sailors. Boys were expected to keep to themselves – they were expected to respect their seniors, and some of the Able Seamen really expected it too. Mere Able Seamen.

But anyway, you went in and you got up three-quarters of an hour before the men, got the hoses out, all the brooms out, and the sand, and you scrubbed decks. Now the sailors when they appeared either had the hoses or they scattered the sand, but the seamen boys did the scrubbing, in bare feet, with their trousers rolled up. It didn't matter what the weather – and if you got a feller's scrubber across your feet in the cold you knew what pain was! And then they would squeegee up, and the most unpopular boys, or the most inefficient boys, or the boys that the particular Leading Seaman that day didn't like, would be given the job of swabbing. These were long swabs made of spun yarn, all tied together at the end with a handle, and you'd have to go along the deck like that, getting the surplus water up. The water collected in the scuppers, so you had to get them along the scuppers and then wring these things out down the actual scupper drain itself, and that again in cold weather was not funny.

But we were looked after in as much as they were all constantly interested in what was happening at home; made you write letters; they saw the food was good; you had access to your divisional officer all the time. But also aboard the *Hood* we were very lucky because we had a Commander (*second in command to the Captain, in charge of day-to-day running of the ship*) by the name of Rory O'Conor, who was killed subsequently aboard the *Neptune*. The door of his cabin was always open. When you joined the ship he gave you a lecture about the *Hood*, and he gave you ten commandments as to what you should and shouldn't do. Anybody could knock on his cabin door and go in and tell him if they had problems. Now that's quite remarkable.

People have said to me it was fatal to complain

No, I don't think that's true. In certain circumstances it could be, but I don't think that's true generally speaking – not in the ships I served in. Not in the *Hood*. The other thing O'Conor insisted on was normally when officers walked around the messdecks in the evening they would expect the men to stand up, but aboard the *Hood* he insisted they walked round the ship with their caps under their arm which meant that nobody was to stand up. This sort of thing. So perhaps he was unusual.[1] There were minor complaints, but people didn't complain much in those days; they put up with things. If there was a bit of injustice you tended to shrug your shoulders and say well that's the way it is.

At the age of eighteen you became an Ordinary Seaman, and even when you went into a men's mess you had to conform to the hierarchy. For example, every messdeck in the big ships had a long table, and a boy promoted to Ordinary Seaman was expected to sit down at the bottom of it.

Another thing was that a sailor could always sit in his own

---

[1] O'Conor's ideas were encapsulated in his book *Running a big ship on Ten Commandments* (Portsmouth, Gieves, 1937). He was killed in December 1941 at the age of 42, when his cruiser HMS *Neptune* ran into a minefield off North Africa and capsized with the loss of all but one of her ship's company.

mess with his hat on, but he should never go into another person's mess with his hat on. That mess might be just over there, but he couldn't turn round on his stool and step over with his hat on. These were marks of respect, the way they maintained their standards.

And so you went on from Ordinary Seaman to eventually Able Seaman, going through various training periods all the time – lots of gunnery and seamanship exercises.

Were you impressed by the Hood *when you first went aboard?*

Overawed! The *Hood* at that time was the most efficient ship in the Navy, she'd won all the sports, ack-ack, gunnery competitions, the manoeuvres competition. She was reckoned to be *it*. I steamed across Portsmouth harbour in a picket boat, and there was this magnificent ship. You've seen pictures – she was the most beautiful thing you'd ever seen, or at least *I'd* ever seen, on water. And I went up the gangway carrying my kitbag, and my hammock; this great sloping gangway; and I looked up and I couldn't believe it – she was enormous.

But she was extremely happy – the boys were a happy crowd; so were the men. They were always organizing competitions with other ships. It's very difficult to describe, that feeling of joining a first ship.

When we went to sea for the first time she began to roll – I didn't think a big thing like that could roll. We headed into a very heavy storm, and this was remarkable to me because I turned in, woke up in the morning in the hammock, banging against the next fellow, and everything was creaking. And as I got out the table came up to meet me, because I was slung above a mess table. I went up to the upper deck and looked out, and I just couldn't believe what I was seeing – this enormous thing was digging her nose in, and throwing the sea right over the top. Behind us were the other battle cruisers *Repulse* and *Renown*, and these things were disappearing – as a wave came up between us they'd totally disappear!

She rolled and she was very wet aft. Even in ordinary weather spray came aft, and when she was going very fast the stern went down and the water actually came over the quarter-deck about that deep. My first feeling about her was that she couldn't be sunk, until the sailors on board told me oh yes she could! And they knew! The ship's sides were eighteen inches thick, with no portholes except for'ard and aft, but horizontally she was thin – for speed you see. Now when I joined the *Nelson*, some time later at the beginning of the war, the decks were about that thick – you would walk along them and they would be chamfered up with another layer, and another layer . . .

When the *Hood* went it was a tremendous blow to all of us. I'd known her a long time then.

What was your job on board the Hood?

I was allocated to the after part of the ship for seamanship and cleaning duties, that's the quarterdeck, and I was a loading number on one of the 5.5 inch guns. But they switched you around a bit.

My greatest impression I think of the *Hood* is when she first fired her 15 inch, because I was told that day with another fellow to go up as communication numbers on the 4 inch ack-ack which was on the boat deck. We left Gibraltar for a night shoot, and it was just dusk, and the after turrets began to train round like this, so that we were looking at the muzzles, at an angle – then they opened fire. I was terrified! Every time the heavy guns fired the whole ship reverberated, it went sideways in fact. That made a terrific impression on me, those guns. But after that I got used to it. Do you know, you can watch 15 inch shells in the air. If we were doing a gunnery shoot, and not closed up ourselves, you could look at a certain point in the sky and you'd see two dots go whooosh, like that! Just two dots. And then you'd see the splashes miles away. You were given nothing to protect your ears except cotton wool, so you went into these RN practices with just bits of cotton wool in your ears, nothing else. I have very happy memories of the *Hood* – I think almost every sailor who served aboard her did.

My next ship was HMS *Exmouth*, an 'E' class destroyer. This was the thing about the Navy – you got a lot of experience, in as much as you could go from a big ship to a small ship, and back to a big ship again. She took a lot of getting used to, and I was terribly seasick first off because the weather was so bad – I remember sleeping underneath a gun shield with a bit of canvas over me, absolutely freezing. Dreadful. I had only felt seasick aboard the *Hood* on one occasion, and that was when it was so rough they had lifelines all round the ship and the Commander piped down – he said only the duty part of the watch remain on deck. But going to a destroyer. Now I knew about this really, because my father had told me – my father fought at Dogger Bank and Jutland, in destroyers – but you don't believe them. I got very sick aboard.

Did they do anything for you?

No. [laughs] when I joined the destroyer we came out of Portsmouth harbour, cleared the Isle of Wight, and an old sailor said to me 'look at that lot!' and he pointed to the horizon – you could see the seas – and a PO [Petty Officer] came up to me and he said 'Here you are, son. There's a block fouled at the top of the mast – go up and clear it, will you?' Now the ship by this time was rolling like a pig, but I got up and I cleared it, and when I came down he said to me 'Well done, you can go down the tiller flat for a smoke'. The tiller flat was right in the stern of the ship, where there was a big engine which moved the rudder. You went down a vertical ladder, and it was a horrible place. I got terribly ill down there, so I came back up, and this PO said 'What's up, son, don't you feel well?' I said 'No'. 'Best thing for you is go and help in the officers' galley.' God! But he wasn't doing it to be difficult, he was trying to get me used to it – giving me the worst possible conditions! I felt dreadful, but they were pretty understanding. I never heard anybody get into trouble or being clipped round the ear, or being ticked off or laughed at for being seasick.

After the *Exmouth* I helped to take the old *Iron Duke*, which was the flagship at Jutland, up to Scapa Flow. We still had her as a training ship, helping to train boys, and we went up to Scapa two days before war broke out. Then I was transferred to the battleship *Nelson* the same day war was declared. It was a very odd feeling – war was declared while we were at sea. By that time I think I was an AB [Able Seaman], and we were cruising out in the North Sea when Chamberlain came on, war with Germany. I had a terrible, terrible feeling of doom. I thought my God, it's war. It suddenly hit me – and of course we'd heard all the arguments about ships being obliterated by air power. There were those who said, 'Oh, ships won't stand a chance'; and others said that with our modern pom-poms and this, that and the other – didn't have radar, but all the other equipment – we'd be OK. But there was always that feeling in the back of your mind.

Tom Dyson was at another boy's training establishment, HMS *Ganges* at Shotley, when war broke out. The role of youngsters like him and his classmates immediately became the subject of speculation.

There was a buzz going round that all us boys would be sent on indefinite leave, until we became eighteen, which was the age you became an Ordinary Seaman. I was seventeen in August 1939, so I'd thought I'd have getting on for a year to wait. But of course it didn't happen. After a bit the buzz went round again – no indefinite leave, that's all rumour; we're definitely going to get drafted.

So sure enough, after we'd finished our training, up went the drafting notice. I think it was about twenty boys drafted to HMS *Caledon*, and twenty to HMS *Calypso*. I wrote home and told my mum I'd been drafted but that I didn't know where I was going. The whole gang of us, forty boys altogether – some from the advanced class and some GC, just a mixture – with a Petty Officer in charge went up by train to Achnasheen. Then we got in a couple of buses which took us the rest of the way to Loch Ewe, where the railway didn't go. The *Caledon* was an old cruiser, and she was crewed by a lot of Royal Fleet Reserve men – in other words, people who had done their time and were on the Fleet Reserve, not weekenders. But they were all a little bit ancient, shall we say, compared with us. Though I don't suppose any of them were much over forty.

The chap in charge of the boys' messdeck was a Leading Seaman; a good man; and the actual lower deck man in charge of us completely was a CPO [Chief Petty Officer] physical and recreational training instructor, who was a very hard man – you had to do what you were told, and you had to do it properly.

We got on board and were assigned our various duties – you

get various duties for the various things the ship's doing, like leaving harbour you'll be such-and-such, coming to anchor or coming to a buoy something else, and closed up for gunnery something else again. One of my jobs was as No.8 on one of her 6 inch guns, that was as a cordite carrier. I wasn't very big, although I was quite strong, and it was my job to stand behind No.6 – there was nine in the gun's crew – and when the gun was being loaded I had to run over to where the cordite charges were coming up, get another one, and come back and stand behind ready with the next one. The biggest fright of my life [laughs] was when the gun first fired. It was a night shoot off Newcastle – I didn't know whether I was coming or going, because the gun just came back at me, and there was all this smell of cordite and bits floating in the air. Of course we had no proper ear plugs or nothing; we had antiflash gear which was worn during wartime and covered all except the circle of your face, but apart from that we didn't have much at all.

I think we went from Loch Ewe to Scapa Flow, where I only went ashore once, to see an ENSA show with Jack Hylton. My first real trip at sea was a patrol from the Faeroes across to Norway, terrible trip. Generally on patrol the boys' job was as lookouts – you stood there, frozen solid, just looking into pitch blackness. When we joined the ship, we were taken round quite a few times, to make sure we knew where we were in the dark. We had a terrible trip; the ship leaked, and we never found nothing. This was another thing, we got very little information. Nothing like you see on the films now, 'This is the Captain speaking . . .', not on the *Caledon*.

Some Captains did

Some Captains did, but they were on the more modern ships. We didn't have a tannoy, our orders were all passed by bosun's call – when the orders were given you got two or three people going round the ship, and they'd just stand at the top of the hatch, stick their head down and blow and shout whatever order was wanted.

We'd had a bit of a bashing, we had some loose plates as well, because we got reriveted. We came down to Swan Hunter's in Wallsend and had a refit and repairs done to the ship. I always remember seeing the riveters, one holding it in one side and the other using the riveting hammer. The buzz went around that we weren't a seaworthy enough ship to remain on the northern patrols, the seas were too heavy. After all, the *Caledon* had been built in 1916.

They decided to send us to the Mediterranean, so we spent Christmas Day in Gibraltar, and New Year's Day 1940 in Malta. We visited Haifa and we went to Cyprus, Malta a lot; we used to live well. Until France collapsed, and things started to go wrong a bit. Our CPO – he was a First World War man – he put his head in his hands and cried, and said to think we went through all that, all to have this happen now.

Not everyone joined as boys, however. The Navy was a large and complex organization, requiring the knowledge and skills of a wide range of specialists. *George Thomas*, a graduate of Nottingham University, joined the RN as a qualified teacher.

I joined the Navy as a schoolmaster in 1938, because I knew that a war was coming. I had already done three years in teaching in a school, which wasn't to my liking, so when I saw an advert in the paper I decided to reply to it, went for an interview at the Admiralty and was accepted. I did the usual preliminary training courses, and was drafted to HMS *Penelope*.

I had to meet the Captain the next morning, and I went up to see him and he said 'Have you been to sea in wartime before?' I said 'No'. He said 'Neither have I!' I thought, well that's a good start. But he turned out to be a very good Captain.

I found life in the Navy quite different from ordinary teaching – they expect you to do a great deal more than just teach sailors. For instance, I was concerned on the *Penelope* with plotting. You're up in the charthouse, with a couple of sailors to help you, and you have big charts on the wall, and you also have a plotting table where you put the chart of the area you're in. Every night when we were in the Atlantic, for instance, the Admiralty used to send us sets of signals in code giving dispositions, or expected dispositions, of U-boats. Those all had to be plotted on the Atlantic chart on the wall, and when it was ready – usually about seven or eight in the evening – the Captain would come down to have a look at it, and I had to explain it all to him; where things had moved from the previous day, and all that.

I shared a cabin at first with the shipwright, but later on I had my own cabin. The hours at sea were twenty-four hours a day – the Captain said to me once 'You know, there are only three people in this ship that work all the time when they go to sea. I'm one, the navigator's another, and you're the third!' I used to take all my gear, change of clothes and so on, up to the plotting office which had a bed in it, back of the compass platform, and I'd stay there the whole time we were at sea. Then come back to my cabin in the stern of the ship when we got into harbour.

You got your sleep when you could. Usually you had your meals brought up to you, and you just had to keep a watch on things all the time. I had two ratings with me who were very competent people, so if it was quiet I'd just say 'Well, you keep an eye on the plot, I'm going to get my head down for a couple of hours.' But there's no real relaxation when you're at sea, not in wartime.

In 1941 we were switched to the Mediterranean and formed part of Force K, with another cruiser, the *Aurora*, and two destroyers, *Lance* and *Lively*. The reason we were sent down there was to attack the convoys going across from Italy to the North African coast, in which we were very successful. The 9 November sticks in my mind, we met an Italian convoy of ten merchant ships and we sank the lot! And the destoyers *Fulmine* and *Libbecio*. And damaged a third destroyer. I remember standing looking at it. I always had a feeling, you know, those poor chaps over there, on the other side. I always had that feeling and I think most people did in the service. Their convoy was overwhelmed by a couple of 6 inch gun cruisers. Our torpedo officer shouted down the voice pipe 'Come up here, Schoolie, and look at this lot!' And I remember going up on the compass platform and seeing all these fires all round. It was dreadful, dreadful. But there it is. That was only one incident out of a number round about that time, and we finished up in the Malta area protecting convoys coming from Alexandria to Malta. We'd come from Malta, sometimes on our own, sometimes bringing empty ships back, and when we got level with Benghazi we'd meet the full ships coming up from Alex, also escorted. We would then take over the ships coming from Alex and they would take over the empties that we'd brought with us, and during all this turning and turning about it was absolute chaos as far as the plotting office was concerned – because we had to turn around and go back again and they had to turn around and go back again, so ships were going in all directions. And at the same time the enemy was sending everything he'd got over in the way of aircraft.

Not even Malta, *Penelope*'s base, offered any real protection against the constant harassment. One raid damaged the ship while she was alongside in Dockyard Creek.

When I got back to the ship my cabin had been virtually destroyed – I couldn't use it, because there'd been a fire. With all this going on, I slept in an air raid shelter ashore! Several of us did! Another ship which was hit, a destroyer just astern of us, took a direct hit and there was a terrific explosion. All I saw was this smoke and stuff going up where this ship had been, and when the smoke had cleared away there was nothing left – just a lot of rubbish on the top of the water. I helped fish the Captain out. He'd broken his leg, that's all, so we got him over to the hospital.

And there were one or two other ships direct hits as well. They were after the merchant ships which we'd brought in from Alexandria – the *Clan Campbell* had been sunk half way to Malta, which left the *Breconshire*, the *Talabot*, and I can't remember the name of the third. The *Breconshire* was hit just offshore, and they had to beach her in one of the bays, but we got the other two into harbour. Malta was almost on its last legs then as far as food was concerned. And these ships had brought all sorts of things like condensed milk, powdered eggs and goodness knows what, for the civilian population, so the Germans and Italians made a special effort to attack them. All hell was let loose while they were in the harbour.

Then they told us there was no good *Penelope* staying there because we'd just be sunk in the harbour too – the best thing was to get out. We were being bombed all the time we were preparing for sea, and in fact the gunnery officer was killed at the last moment – just as we were on the point of sailing a bomb dropped nearby, near the compass platform, and he was hit by some of the shrapnel. The bomb broke up, bits flying all over the place. We sailed I suppose about seven o'clock that evening, hoping to get far enough away from Malta by daylight to escape further raids, but they came after us – they knew we were trying to get away from Malta. But we managed it. We went straight into dry dock at Gibraltar, because the ship would have sunk alongside, she was so full of holes.

So extensive was the damage sustained by the *Penelope* that the wags of the lower deck coined the nickname HMS *Pepperpot*.

That was my wartime effort as far as sea time was concerned – it was all crammed into eight months, nine months. Then they pulled me out of the ship because they said she had to be repaired in New York, and they wanted me back in England.

What kind of subjects were you teaching in the Navy?

To start with, if you were on a general list as a new recruit, you would do things like elementary mathematics, because sailors weren't very good at that sort of thing. I went to Shotley, which is where boys first joined the Navy, and did ordinary teaching there – the history of the Navy, mathematics, a little bit of navigation; very elementary stuff. But quite a lot of the instructors had specialized knowledge – in my case, physics – and expressed a preference, so when I came back from *Penelope* I was picked out to go and take over a small school in Chatham which was for minesweeping personnel.

It was essentially concerned with the theory of magnetic mines, and the degaussing cables they put round the ships, and why they stopped magnetic mines from going off. While I was there the opportunity arose of taking City and Guilds examinations in electrical engineering. This was one of the schemes which the Navy ran right through the war, operated from HMS *Vernon* at Portsmouth. I did the studying for this in my spare time, eventually took the examinations, and qualified to the extent that the Institute of Electrical Engineers accepted me as

an associate member. From then on I was almost entirely concerned in my shore work with electrical topics, and I finished
up teaching degree students in Greenwich.

The seamen were responsible for the more traditional tasks on
board ship, for handling the vessel, and for crewing her boats and
her armament. But down below, in the boiler and engine rooms and
the machinery spaces, the other large block making up each ship's
company – the stokers – held sway.

Ralph Farrell served as a stoker on one of the fleet's bigger ships,
the battle cruiser *Renown*.

We were basically there to operate the fuel valves. You were
cheap labour. They didn't need half the number of people that
were down there. In a boiler room on the *Renown* you would
have perhaps eight boilers – each stoker would have two to
look after with maybe six sprayers on each. There'd be a Stoker
Petty Officer there watching the steam gauges and he'd go with
his finger 'Up one' – and you'd immediately put another
sprayer on – 'Down one' – and you had to do the business of
shutting the air flaps again. By today's standards ships were
hopelessly overmanned, and all of these people had to be found
jobs. The amount of time you spent in futile occupations like
cleaning brass and holystoning decks. Well, it wasn't totally
futile I suppose – in a sense it gave you a pride in appearance.
But they were overmanned. I've no doubt at all in the days of
coal-fired boilers you needed them, but you could put on three
[*fuel oil*] sprayers in three seconds. It was as easy as that. Then
you just stood around doing nothing for hours until it was time
to shut them down again. You'd have to go up and walk round
the fan flap and see if the fans had their oil in them, this sort of
thing. Mind you, probably in wartime there was justification
for it – you needed replacements, and people would be ill.

*What did you think of the machinery you were working
with?*

It was pre-war British machinery, and you couldn't say more
than that!

When I went to the *Suffolk* I got to know every inch of that
bloody thing. She wasn't that old, built about 1928, but she got

a hell of a pounding. They were treated unmercifully, run into the ground more or less, and after a while with all this sea time your rivets all leaked, left, right and centre. Although it was nothing serious, you had all this seepage of water into the fuel tanks and you also had seepage of oil out. So you'd leave a bit of a trail behind. All our fuel tanks had water in them, so they appointed me to go into each oil tank in turn to saw a foot off the oil suction pipes so we sucked up oil instead of seawater – which is a bit pointless, because the water eventually got up that foot anyway!

Making sure all this technology worked was the responsibility of a smaller group on board – the engine room artificers, or ERAs. *Bill Kellie* recalls being sent to a destroyer at Malta to gain some experience:

She was lying in Dockyard Creek, Senglea. I humped my kit-bag, hammock and suitcase up the boarding ladder and reported to the sentry, who took me to the ERA's mess. This was on the port side, just for'ard of the break. You entered it through a round hatch in the deck, and down an almost vertical ladder to the lower deck, which was just below the waterline. The mess was fifteen feet by ten feet; there were three portholes, always battened shut whilst at sea, three seat lockers along each side with a table in between them, and two cupboards for provisions and cooking utensils. In one corner was the hammock rack where our hammocks were stored during the day. This was the living quarters for six people – here we ate, slept, stowed all our kit and private belongings and learned how to live together and tolerate each other's foibles. Harmony in such cramped quarters, under the tensions and stresses of war, was of vital importance to all the occupants. Which were: a Chief ERA, three watchkeeping ERA's, one trainee ERA – me – and a First Class Stoker as mess man.

The mess consisted of 'Chiefy' who was Gerry, a native of Plymouth who had joined the RN in 1916 as a boy entrant and was due to be pensioned off when the war became imminent. His constant wonder was, would he ever draw his pension. The senior watchkeeper was Reg, also from Plymouth and a boy entrant in 1932. He was waiting to sit the exam for Chief ERA. The others were Jacka, from Teignmouth, and Jackie, from Stoke-on-Trent, who had both joined as tradesmen. The mess man, constantly singing country and western type tunes and known as Buckskin Pete, was a Geordie from Chester-le-Street.

Defender was having a number of defects rectified, and was not due to leave the dockyard for another two weeks. Our sister ship *Duchess* left after two days on her way to the Clyde for a major refit – they would be home for Christmas, lucky so-and-sos. How I wished I had signed on for her when given the chance, instead of my mate Bob Kinninmont.

I spent my days becoming familiar with the layout of the ship. She was very little different to HMS *Blanche* or *Boadicea* on which I had worked whilst serving my apprenticeship at Hawthorn Leslie's on the Tyne. My spare time I spent exploring Malta.

The refit completed, we sailed at dusk one evening. Dawn found us at action stations. Every day at sea all ships greeted the dawn at action stations – these lasted from half an hour before daybreak to half an hour afterwards. We were escorting a convoy of troop ships bound for Alexandria. The voyage was uneventful until we reached our destination, but as the merchant ships entered harbour we picked up an echo on the Asdic gear thought to be a submarine. We closed up to action stations – my place was with the after fire and repair party.

With two other destroyers we circled and criss-crossed the area of the contact dropping patterns of depth charges. But though we hung around for some time, contact had been lost so we entered harbour three hours later.

We oiled and left the following day for Port Said, where we picked up a mixed group of merchant ships westbound for Gibraltar. We delivered them after an uneventful voyage to the care of another escort while we changed over to a convoy bound for Malta, which we had been told was again to be our base. October and November passed with us steaming constantly east or west in the Mediterranean. We were due for a boiler clean – at that time this was done after 500 hours steaming – but there was such a shortage of destroyers and escort vessels in the area that this period had to be extended.

Mid-December I was sent to the gunnery school, shown how to use a naval cutlass and how to load and fire a .45 revolver, though I never fired a shot. The training course lasted for three hours – very comprehensive!

Just before we put to sea, I received a short letter from my wife Gladys telling me that she had given birth to a baby boy; all was well with her and the baby but she was tired and would write a longer letter with all the news when she was rested.

After two days at sea I discovered why I had attended the gunnery school. We were proceeding to the Dardanelles on contraband control, and I was to be a member of the boarding party. My duty when we boarded a ship was to take charge of the engine room while the search was in progress. In charge of the boarding party was the First Lieutenant. He was to be the first up the ladder, armed with a revolver and a whistle – I never did find out what the whistle signals were. Then I was to be next up the ladder, followed by the four seamen, also armed with revolvers and cutlasses. We were told that should there be any resistance we were to use our weapons. If we lost the Lieutenant I was to take over the operation. It sounded a bit like Fred Karno's Army to me, but we were given a small box of six cartridges each and practised shooting and loading our revolvers. The targets were bottles towed in the wake of the ship. I became quite proficient – or at least I felt more capable of using the revolver. As for the cutlass . . .

On arrival at the entrance to the Dardanelles we took over the patrol from another destroyer, exchanged greetings; she wished us good luck and left for Malta. We proceeded to steam back and forth at the entrance, just outside the three-mile limit. We had to proceed at the most economical speed possible; this meant one boiler lit up, a second warmed through ready for immediate light up, one turbine running and the other ready for use if required. Our speed was three knots – a walking pace. If the weather was bad and the sea rough, this was a most uncomfortable speed to maintain. And as we slowly consumed our oil, the size of the roll and the discomfort increased. There was a constant stream of seasick men to the lee side. Luckily I was free from that ailment.

Below and above decks everything had to be secured. In our

mess the mess man, Buckskin Pete, had dropped a bag of dried peas which had burst, and the sound of these rolling back and forth from under the lockers was a lullaby we could have done without. Eventually they were all cleared up. The days passed slowly – the ships we hailed gave full particulars of the cargoes they were carrying and where bound; these were checked against information we had on board, and all were cleared. The boarding party, though at the ready, were never required to board any vessels, until one day we stopped a small sailing caique.

She carried her cargo in two holds which were covered by tarpaulins. Her skipper spoke no English, and our Captain insisted that the First Lieutenant went aboard her and made the crew remove the covers over the cargo, so that we could inspect the contents of the holds. As soon as one corner of the tarpaulin had been rolled back it was obvious what she was carrying, the stench was dreadful. She was fully loaded with a cargo of human and animal excrement – manure for one of the Greek islands! We moved immediately to windward. Our skipper made some seamen poke this stuff with long metal rods, searching for anything buried beneath it. Nothing was found, so they were allowed to proceed on their voyage.

Around this time we were given the news that our sister ship HMS *Duchess*, whilst entering the Firth of Clyde, had been run down during the middle watch by HMS *Barham*, the battleship she was escorting. She had rolled over and sunk immediately – the only survivors were the watch on deck, twenty-three men. I went cold when I heard this news, realizing how close I had been to death when I had almost signed on for her. Bob would not have been on deck, he would have been either on watch in a boiler room or asleep in the mess. Maybe that nightmare he had had when we were training – which woke him one night yelling and screaming – and never told us about had come true.

We spent Christmas and New Year at sea that year, but managed to celebrate in a half-hearted manner as best we could. Most of our thoughts were of home. We returned to Malta after five weeks on station, oiled ship, provisioned and left again for another five weeks contraband patrol. The weather was dreadful – it was bitterly cold; each day it was either rain, sleet or snow, or a mixture of all three. The whole ship felt cold. Then it was found that the flour we had loaded in Malta was infested with weevils. Each new batch of bread that the cook baked seemed to have more dead weevils than the previous batch. At first most of the crew picked out the weevils in a slice of bread, then it was decided to call the black spots 'caraway seeds'. Not that that improved their flavour. Then the surgeon said that as they had been baked, they were sterilized and became fresh killed baked meat – they were full of protein and would be a healthy addition to our diet!

During this cold spell cockroaches, huge horrible-looking creatures that appeared to watch you as they waved their antennae around searching for food – *Defender* had brought them from China – now began to appear from all sorts of nooks and crannies in which they had been hiding. The cold killed them quickly, but the snag was that they always seemed to fall from the deckhead into your cup of tea, into your soup, on your bread and jam or on your dinner plate. They were difficult to ignore, and no one seemed to acquire a taste for them, no matter what propaganda the surgeon spread.

At least this time we did have a very successful trip. After five weeks at sea we hailed and stopped a fully-laden Norwegian oil tanker. They lowered a ladder for us to board; the Lieutenant was first up, I was close behind, followed by the seamen. I made my way down to the manoeuvring platform in the engine room. The engine, a diesel, was stopped. I gestured to one man to move away from the controls, and assumed command of the engine room. A few minutes later the phone rang from the bridge – it was the Lieutenant, asking if the Captain was down there. He hung up when I replied that he was not in the engine room. Just then a man appeared from behind the engine, wearing a clean white boiler suit. He seemed huge, so when he began to move towards me I called out in English for him to stand back. He said nothing, but continued to approach me, and now I was scared! I motioned to him to keep away, drew my revolver from its holster and levelled it at him. With that he stood still. I was in a cold sweat – I thought, 'if he comes any closer I'll have to shoot him'. My legs began to tremble. Just then the phone rang again, and again it was the Lieutenant enquiring after the Captain. I told him I had a very threatening person beside me but I would give him the phone, as he might know the whereabouts of the Captain. Motioning to this fellow that I wanted him to take the telephone, I laid it on the deck and moved back from the controls. He picked it up and said, in perfect English, 'This is the Captain speaking, and as soon as I am allowed I shall return to the bridge'.

This utterly deflated me. I never spoke, but waved the gun towards the ladder leading to the deck, and he climbed out of the engine room. No one else was near me, so I replaced my revolver in the holster and relaxed. As I was fumbling to get the gun fastened into the holster it dawned on me that I had never released the safety catch on the weapon! What if I had had to use it?

The cargo of oil we discovered was being shipped to Bremen, so it was impounded and instead delivered to Malta. Three of us were left on board as a prize crew, and after hoisting the White Ensign accompanied the tanker to her new destination. We were well looked after by the Norwegians on the passage to Malta – they all seemed well pleased the cargo wouldn't be used by the Germans. We lived and fed with the officers, and never whilst sitting at the table with the Captain did I mention the safety catch episode.

We rejoined *Defender* when she arrived in the dockyard. Our next trip was to Gibraltar with four tankers, one of them the ship we had taken over, and on arrival the off-duty watch was granted shore leave. After a couple of beers I went to the cinema, I forget the name of the film that was showing, but during the performance there was flashed on the screen '*Defender*'s ship's company – return to the ship at once'. One hour later we left the harbour with two boilers steaming and the third warming through, and steered a course due west through the straits into the teeth of a full gale blowing in from the Atlantic. On the third boiler reaching full pressure the main stop valves were opened, the boiler was connected to the main steam line and we increased to full speed.

At midnight the watch changed and I had to get to the engine room. Safety lines had been rigged along the upper deck with grab strops hanging from them should anyone be caught by a sea sweeping across the deck. Clutching a grab strop I made my way from the shelter of the bridge to the engine room hatch. It truly was a wild night. At the first chance I flung the hatch open, jumped through and on to the ladder, but before I had time to close and lock the hatch a shower of salt water followed me down.

Over the tannoy came a message that there was to be no more movement along the upper deck until further notice. We were going to the assistance of a merchant ship in difficulty 300 miles west of Oporto, and expected to rendezvous with her at 0800.

We sighted the crippled ship just after 0830 – her engine had broken down and she was drifting. We circled slowly around her keeping an antisubmarine watch with our Asdic gear for the next thirty hours, till a tug arrived to take her in tow. A line was passed between them, then the towing hawser, and then they began to move, but there was a sudden commotion aboard the tug. Using her loud hailer the tug requested medical help, as she had a man injured.

We lowered the whaler on the lee side, a difficult operation in the heavy seas, and the surgeon went aboard the tug. We were told later that a man had been trapped between the towing hawser and the ship's side by a sudden yaw of the tug in the heavy seas as she commenced the tow – he died from his injuries, and was buried at sea.

The high speed run had consumed a large percentage of our fuel and we were now very short of oil, so another destroyer relieved us and we returned to Gib. The return trip was much quieter. We were steaming with a large stern sea under our quarter, and the old sailor's adage of 'No one's ever sick in a stern sea' proved correct – the movement of the ship made you very sleepy.

As soon as we had oiled and provisioned ship we put to sea again. This time the buzz was that we were heading for Devonport, but at the entrance to the straits we altered course to south-west by south, heading into the South Atlantic and away from the UK. So much for wishful thinking. Our destination turned out to be Freetown, Sierra Leone, where our task was to hunt for an armed raider making the passage to Germany.

We spent a number of weeks prowling at economical speed between South America and West Africa but without success. Between sea trips we were allowed some time ashore. Freetown seemed a broken down, large straggling place – very few buildings of note or substance, and nothing to recommend it at all. I took a steam train which ran on a single track to a town called Waterloo about twenty miles inland, but this turned out to be a conglomeration of grass shacks where the main pastimes of the inhabitants seemed to be selling fruit and gazing at visitors open mouthed. Freetown was a thriving metropolis by comparison.

Dakar, Senegal, was our next port of call. We found that we required some assistance from the French naval dockyard with the repair of a feed pump. Happily Dakar proved to be completely different in every way from Freetown, and one thing I always remember was a mountain of peanuts on the quayside. The heap must have been thirty feet high, fifty feet wide, and stretched for over a hundred yards. When we left, every mess had a huge store of peanuts, brought aboard as we returned to the ship. We were eating peanuts for months afterwards.

We were moored alongside a French naval vessel, the *D'Entrecasteaux*. She also was having some minor defects repaired, and we became very friendly with her engine room staff. Visits were exchanged, and the night before our departure as many as could be spared from duty had a run ashore together. The armed raider had escaped the hunters, and we left the following morning for Gib., en route to our home base at Malta.

Whilst alongside an oiler in Grand Harbour being refuelled we heard over the radio that hostilities had flared up. Holland and Belgium had been attacked, and the blitzkrieg had begun in earnest. We all felt sure that the French Maginot Line would stop the advance. We were on a run to Alexandria when we heard of the evacuation from Dunkirk, and then the capitulation of France. On arrival in harbour the Captain cleared lower deck, and when we were all assembled told us there was every possibility that an attempt would be made to invade and subdue the UK. We wouldn't surrender – if necessary the ship would proceed to Canada and operate from there. We all gave a half-hearted cheer when he'd finished, but I doubt anyone felt very heroic. A last-ditch stand sounded fine in an adventure yarn, but this was for real.

On the way back to Malta with our next convoy we heard that Italy had now declared war on us. This altered the whole situation in the Med., because now we could expect the Italian Navy and Air Force to intervene. The following day we were piped to action stations, air raid alert. We had closed up for action, awaiting developments, when suddenly there was a string of bomb splashes about two miles from the starboard side of the convoy. I looked but could see no aircraft with the naked eye, so they must have bombed from an extremely high altitude. Some few seconds later we felt and heard the thud of the explosions against the hull. We had a number of alarms during the short period before we entered Grand Harbour, almost all with the same result – no damage to the convoy. But we did once fire a few anti-aircraft rounds.

News from home became mostly about air raids. Coventry and Plymouth had been almost destroyed. Mail deliveries from the UK were so irregular. In one letter Gladys told me she'd cancelled the insurance policy – when she'd asked about the exemption clause the agent said it didn't mean they wouldn't meet their commitments, but he couldn't give any written agreement that war risks would be included! *Defender* was a Devonport-manned ship, and many of the men with homes in that area were anxiously awaiting news of their families. With the main Rolls-Royce engine factory being at Derby, my fears were for Gladys and the two babies. I felt sure that Derby would be blitzed.

Little effort was made to make shipboard life less onerous for the crews, and facilities, even aboard the newer ships, remained extremely basic.

Roy Bennett was serving aboard the cruiser HMS *Southampton* when war broke out.

It probably seems a bit unreal now. To start with, food was prepared by the stokers and seamen themselves, and the cooks only cooked it. There were no showers, no baths – only a tank with water heated by a steam coil and an enamel bowl. You slept in hammocks which were so close together you could hardly squeeze between. Clothes were washed in a bucket and dried in a machinery space! The Naval Discipline Act was read at every major punishment – the person at attention between guards and everyone with caps removed – and at other times whenever the Captain decided to assemble the ship's company. When you hear constantly 'Death or such other punishment as hereafter mentioned' it's very effective!

Everyone knew what they had to do and everyone normally did it. Everyone obeyed instructions from those above them in rank.

When the war came along, leave and shore time virtually ceased for those of us who served in ships. Additional to our normal working, all time off watch was at damage control stations in various states of alert depending on the operation, area or action. Half or even three-quarters of a ship's complement were likely to be untrained by peacetime standards, throwing all the extra work on key people. Food was awful, with very little of it fresh due to sea time. And each man's living space became even smaller due to increased wartime complements and the need to pack in stores and new types of equipment.

It was a similar story aboard the *Glasgow*, as *John Kelleher* recalls:

You would have a crew which was right up to strength, if not over strength, and so in a ship like the *Glasgow* there would be something like 750 altogether including officers; we all lived in very cramped conditions. The crew used hammocks to sleep in – it was only the officers who used bunks. Hammocks weren't an uncomfortable way of sleeping but they did involve quite a bit of physical preparation and wrapping up afterwards. Before you turned in you had to sling your hammock, which meant you had to get it and physically sling it between two hooks in the mess; unwrap it, and prepare the blankets and so on; and then finally you climbed in. When you were roused in the morning you had to do the reverse, and lash up the hammock and stow it away – they doubled as damage control material in the event that the ship was holed.

Another uncomfortable thing was that during wartime you had to be prepared at all times, so you had to take your gas mask and antiflash gear with you wherever you went on the ship. If you were at sea during wartime, they had a routine whereby a half an hour before dawn the ship would go to action stations, the reason for this being that visibility suddenly increases at dawn, and you could be subject to a surprise attack. This meant rising at some ungodly hour from about half past four in the morning onwards, depending on when dawn occurred, going to your action station, complete with overalls on and your antiflash gear, your gas mask, and in the case of an artificer a tool box, and staying there until you were stood down, so it could mean an hour. Typically my action stations were in very uncomfortable places in the ship, for instance at one time it was in a diesel dynamo room. So you were in a room where there was a large diesel engine driving a dynamo, with the attendant noise and vibration, and you had to stay on the end of a special phone until you were told to stand down.

The food was very basic and often badly cooked – one of the disciplines that you learned in the Navy was to get by on unsatisfactory food. The thing that helped a lot of people including myself was the tot of rum that we had every day, because that acted as an appetizer and made it easier to eat food which otherwise seemed to be very unpalatable. Leisure facilities were very few indeed. We were more or less packed like sardines, so they mainly consisted of reading, writing, playing cards and such sedentary pastimes. There just wasn't room for any other kinds of games or physical activities. When you were in port you used the time to go ashore, drink a lot of beer, have a good singsong and get a decent meal – all the things that you were dreaming about when you were at sea. Because apart from the tot you weren't allowed any alcohol, so you used to yearn for time in port so you could go ashore to a bar. Time in port wasn't usually very long, because there was a great demand for ships during the war.

I was on the *Glasgow* for about four years during the war, and I was on a similar ship, the *Liverpool*, for a year after the war was over. They impressed me very much as fighting machines. They both sustained substantial damage from enemy action, as did a number of other Town class cruisers, and in most cases they were able to survive and fight again, so I felt privileged in a way that I was serving on such ships.

I definitely think that my service in the Navy has affected my later life, that's undoubtedly true. I have one abiding thing that I thank the Navy for, and that is the fact that I travelled around the world and saw so many other countries. There were strains during the war, of separation and uncertainty – uncertainty of what was happening at home because of lack of news, and not being in close contact with loved ones. The frequent separations and farewells did impose a strain on people.

The Navy preferred to recruit its officers, like its seamen, at an early age. *Lloyd Davies* was one such youngster, attracted by the lure of the sea.

I decided at an early age that I wanted to join the Royal Navy, so my father swapped me over to a preparatory school near Shrewsbury which had quite a good record of getting people into the RN. There were about 400 people trying to get in when I got in – it was rather popular – and they took about a hundred. The first news I had of my success was when my father received a telegram from Gieves, the naval outfitters, 'Congratulations on your son's success'. I went in at the age of thirteen and a half, first to the Royal Naval College, Osborne. The war was on then – the First World War – and after about a year there we were moved on to Dartmouth, the big new naval college. I had only been there a short time when the Armistice was signed.

The end of the war signalled a period of retrenchment for the Navy as ships were scrapped and men demobilized. The 'Geddes Axe', named after the chairman of a committee on reducing public expenditure, trimmed costs ruthlessly.

Of the hundred, about twenty-five of our term fell victim to the Geddes Axe, mostly for academic reasons. The rest of us stayed on to complete our training and finally went to sea at the age of about seventeen and a half. My first ship as a naval cadet was the battleship HMS *Temeraire*. I did a three months cruise in her, and then they changed the training ship to HMS *Thunderer*. I went to her for three months too, and that completed my six months training as a naval cadet. I then went off as a Midshipman, aged about eighteen, to the battleship *Ramillies*, which was my first proper seagoing ship.

I stayed in the *Ramillies* as a Midshipman for about three years, during which time I went away for three months of destroyer training, and at the end of our time we had an exam, and I managed to come out top of the squadron in that! We were made Acting Sub-Lieutenants, and went off to do our various courses – torpedoes, gunnery, signals, and the Royal Naval College, Greenwich, which was the first of the courses. Then we finally became Sub-Lieutenants, and we went off to sea to complete our training and get what they called our watchkeeping certificate. I spent about a year on a destroyer, appropriately called the *Watchman*, where I got my watchkeeping ticket, then got made up to Lieutenant and moved on to the cruiser HMS *Coventry* as a watchkeeper and general service officer. I was there for about two and a half years. Nothing particular happened, except we won the Mediterranean Fleet regatta! I rowed in the officers' winning crew, which pleased me a lot. By now I had reached the age when you specialized. I was very keen to become a gunnery officer, and I was finally selected, which again pleased me a lot, as gunnery was at that time considered the best thing.

So it was back to Greenwich for six months of mostly gunnery and maths, and then to Whale Island [HMS Excellent – the gunnery school at Portsmouth], where they appointed me to the junior staff. I had some interesting jobs there. Actually I think one of the reasons why I was put on the staff was that each of us had to give a lecture when we were qualifying; mine was on whales, and I decided to make it rather dramatic, so I got some stuff from London from the Whaling Research Association, and plunged on to the platform waving a harpoon. I so impressed everybody, the Admirals and Captains who were listening, that they eventually put me on the junior staff!

I enjoyed my time at Whale Island very much. I was a parade ground officer there for about a year, in charge of training in that type of thing. They also sent me off to the battleship *Valiant* to do the trials of the first multiple pom-pom guns [for anti-aircraft defence]. I spent about three months on that job, and finally sent in my report to the experimental office, Whale Island.

Then, funnily enough, I went back to my old ship, HMS *Coventry*, as gunnery officer. That was a very interesting commission of two and a half years. I remember we once did a night exercise when the ships were all darkened, and of course we didn't have radar in those days, and one of our destroyers came straight for us; they hadn't seen us. We maintained a steady course, she managed to alter course, and she passed so close to us that we were actually looking down on her decks and we could hear the fans going in the boiler room! It was as close as that. After that the flagship ordered the fleet to put on their lights – it was becoming really rather dangerous.

In those days the Mediterranean, which was where we were, was a very happy place. We were based on Malta, and we could go almost anywhere in the Mediterranean and be received with open arms. We spent a lot of time round Greece, and in Yugoslavia. The Egyptian police, who at that time were officered by British officers, taught me how to fight it rough through a house, and things like that. You went into a house, armed with a revolver in each hand, and cardboard figures sprang out at you from various places – you just fired as they came! I went to the wedding of King Farouk, who was the King of Egypt then, and Queen Farida. It was a very spectacular event, and the only time I've ever seen roast peacock – it tastes very much like anything else, like turkey.

I then went back to Whale Island on the staff as a Lieutenant-Commander, in charge of all ratings' training there.

Lieutenant-Commander was the highest an officer advanced on seniority alone. Promotion above this level – to Commander, Captain and then flag rank – required favourable reports by your seniors.

Before the war it was very rough really – only about one in four got to Commander. Of course the war speeded it up because a lot of chaps got killed. You had your confidential reports, you see, which went back to the Admiralty. I think it was in nine headings – things like leadership, officer-like qualities, and they were all rated from 0 to 9. If you got 0 you must have been a real bad character! Nobody ever got 9, but if you got 8s and 7s you were in with a chance. These were done by the Captain of the ship. Of course, having been through them, I was making out ones of my own later on.

What did you look for in an officer?

I don't know; a certain amount of initiative, I suppose. After all, as a Lieutenant in the Navy I was taught that the one thing which was inexcusable was to say you hadn't done something because you hadn't had an order. If you didn't get an order, you used your initiative.

What was Whale Island like? – some former ratings have compared it to Alcatraz!

I found it really rather nice. You had Whale Island all on its own, literally on an island in Portsmouth harbour, connected to the mainland by a footbridge. That made it a very attractive place – you were well away from the Commander-in-chief! You ran your own show. There was a very high morale there. You have to remember that in those days – it's not the same now – but in those days, gunnery officers and the officers at Whale Island in particular considered themselves the cream of the Navy, from the point of view of discipline and everything else.

When I was there there were seventeen officers and only three of them, the Captain and Commander and one other, were married. All the rest were bachelors. In those days you see nobody married in the Navy very much before the age of thirty – you didn't get a marriage allowance until you were thirty; it's different now. In those days, the average chap, unless he had private means, couldn't afford to marry. Which had its good points as well from the point of view of the mess. At guest night all the officers were there – whereas now they have to bulldoze them into it.

Where did you go after this second spell at Whale Island?

Captain Horan, who'd been in the *Coventry* with me and was now Flag Captain of the fleet flagship, HMS *Barham*, in the Mediterranean, asked me to come out there again, and so I went to the *Barham* in 1937 as her gunnery officer. I was quite certain by that time, having been to Germany, that war was coming, and told the Captain so. Consequently a lot of my time was spent in getting the ship ready for war.

When it finally began we were ordered home, as it became clear that the Italians were not at first entering the war, and we went up to join the Home Fleet.

We were coming back from patrol just after Christmas, 28 December, when a U-boat drew a bead on us and got us with one torpedo. We managed to save the ship by closing all the watertight doors, and we got her in finally to Liverpool – they couldn't take us at Glasgow, there was no dock big enough, so they ordered us down to the Gladstone Dock in Liverpool. Six tugs brought us in, as we were very unmanageable because we had 2,500 tons of water on board. When we finally docked I went down to the shell room, and the Captain insisted on coming with me – the Captain by this time was 'Hooky' Walker; he had only one arm. There were about five or six in the shell room dead, but they hadn't been drowned, which was what I was really worried about – as to whether we'd closed the watertight doors too soon, and drowned them. But they were all at their action stations, and it was obvious they'd all been killed by the explosion.

Only about a week after that I was promoted to Commander, and left the ship to go to the Admiralty on the staff of the DNO [Director of Naval Ordnance]. During my two fairly hectic years at the Admiralty I travelled quite a lot, up to Glasgow, to Newcastle; I was sent up to Coventry the day after the blitz there, in order to see how much damage had been done to Admiralty factories.

During that time I also married, Lord Clifton's daughter, though we didn't see much of each other during the war, and on completion of my time at the Admiralty I was sent over to the States for six months, to bring them up to date on everything we'd been doing.

Then I came back as second in command of HMS *Glasgow*. We did one trip up north to the Arctic convoys, which wasn't very pleasant, then we went down to Plymouth and were based there to support the ships and the escort groups in the Atlantic.

We stayed there for some considerable time, before being partly based in the Azores. The only thing about there was we had to have the ship lit up at night, which seemed quite extraordinary! Then as soon as we left harbour we darkened ship again.

We'd arranged to give a children's party there just after Christmas, with a large Christmas tree, when we suddenly got a signal from the Admiralty ordering us to sea to intercept a German blockade runner. We were warned that the German flotillas were out, and we thought we might encounter the Bordeaux flotilla, which consisted of five destroyers. But when we met them there were eleven – the Bordeaux and Brest flotillas had joined up – and we had our most spirited action of the war for me.

We went in and the Yeoman of Signals said 'Enemy in sight'. He started counting them out and there were eleven ships, which rather took the smile off my face. As usual I went aft, to the after control, so that if the ship got badly hit I could take over – the Captain stayed in the for'ard control and I was in the after control, as second in command of the ship. We really didn't know an awful lot of what was going on, we just fired and fired – it was in the hands of the gunnery officer, who got the DSC that day. In the heat of the action the Germans turned towards us and fired torpedoes – we reckoned there were about sixty torpedoes coming for us! So we turned away as fast as we could for the moment, and the nearest torpedo passed us about 400 yards away I think. Then we turned back and went into action again. I think it was at that stage that they gave up to a certain extent. They were making for home, trying to get back into Brest.

We opened fire at about 1.30 and we fought them till 4.30, by which time we'd sunk a big Narvik class destroyer, the Z.27, and two smaller destroyers, the T.25 and T.26, about half the size. We also put four more out of action. In fact we ran out of ammunition, because we'd fired so much. All the paint was peeling off our guns from the heat. We had very few people killed – I think we had one direct hit on one of our pom-poms which killed about four men – and we had a certain number wounded, otherwise the ship's company was fairly unscathed.

As we pulled out the German Air Force came out to attack

us. Fortunately night was closing in so they only had one attack, in which they used glider bombs, and they missed. We had the *Enterprise*, another cruiser, with us, but her main gunnery control equipment broke down in the course of the action, so we fought it very much on our own. We were met by Spitfires off the Scilly Isles and we buried the people who had been killed on board – with wreaths made from the Christmas tree intended for the children of Horta – and went into Plymouth, where we received a terrific reception. The dockyard mateys cheered us all the way.

The yard official at Plymouth said we were too badly damaged to go to sea again – we had lot of holes in the side of the ship from near misses – which was just as well, because they were talking about sending down the ammunition lighters to top us up. As it was we got a fortnight's leave.

With hindsight I think the German ships were very badly handled. They ought to have engaged us all at once. Instead of that I think their thoughts were much more of getting away than of fighting. After all, they had eleven ships there and they should have been able to bring us under very heavy fire, but instead of that we knocked them out one after another. The odds were really heavily against us. I gather that the Admiralty was very pleased with the outcome – though they'd had slightly cold feet when they heard we were fighting them all by ourselves. It had quite an effect on D-Day, because we more or less destroyed the Brest and Bordeaux flotillas as a fighting force. If they'd been intact at the time of D-Day six months later they could have caused a certain amount of mayhem on the beaches.

Young officers who were at an earlier stage in their training when war broke out found their courses shortened to speed up the flow of qualified personnel. *Richard Pridham-Wippel* also found gaining his watchkeeping certificate rather more of an adventure than he had bargained for:

I joined the Royal Naval College, Dartmouth, in 1934 and left at the end of 1937 to follow the usual sort of pattern – went to sea as a cadet at the beginning of 1938; then I served as a Midshipman in two cruisers, one was the *Cornwall*, the other was the *Manchester*. I was only on the *Cornwall* about three months, then I joined the *Manchester* and we went out to the East Indies. We were based at Trincomalee, Ceylon, and our parish in those days was the whole of the Indian Ocean down as far as Singapore, down the African coast as far as Dar es Salaam, including the Red Sea and Persian Gulf. In fact we didn't go to the Gulf on that particular occasion, but it was part of our East Indies Station.

We were in Aden on 3 September 1939, and I remember we got the news – I suppose it must have been in the afternoon as far as we were concerned, about three o'clock or something like that – and we took the tampions [protective muzzle covers] out of the guns and sailed for Bombay almost immediately.

We spent the first three months of the war convoying troops – Indian troops largely – from Bombay; occasionally we would go into Colombo, refuel and provision. We'd take them across the Arabian Sea and up the Red Sea, beyond Massawa and Jiddah, because the Germans had some armed merchant cruisers in those two ports; so we'd get them clear of there, then leave the convoy to go on by itself to Suez while we turned round, refuelled at Aden, and went back for another one. We did that until early December I suppose, and then we were ordered home. We arrived back in actual fact just before Christmas 1939.

Then I became a Sub-Lieutenant and I had to do the technical courses – gunnery, torpedoes, navigation – which were condensed from the usual eighteen months which they used to be, down to about three months. And they had the same syllabus, so it was a bit of a sweat.

I joined the Tribal class destroyer *Ashanti* at Dundee in about April 1940 as a Sub-Lieutenant. She'd just come back from Narvik. We spent the next few months chasing submarines, operating from Scapa, out into the Atlantic, North Sea. We escorted some of the children's convoys going over to Canada and the States. Up to Iceland, in and out of Greenock, Liverpool; general anti submarine work at that time. We had one rather good surface action, which I believe later became known as the Battle of Egero Light, when we went over to Norway. We'd had a report of a German convoy going up the coast, and we made a very good interception at night. The lighthouse on Cape Egero was lit, they lit it for the convoy, and we had a rather short, sharp battle and sank the whole lot. There was one casualty in *Cossack* − a shell hit the tiller flat, and one sailor was killed − but that was the only casualty on our side. Then we beat it like fury back to Rosyth, because we were only a few minutes flying time from Stavanger, where the German Air Force was pretty active. Fortunately it was very low cloud the following day, so we weren't spotted at all and got straight back.

A week later we sailed for Newcastle, because the brand new battleship *King George V* was coming out, having just been built, and our orders were to escort her up to Rosyth. We went down the swept channel − the Germans had started dropping acoustic mines, and the theory in those days was if you steamed fast enough over an acoustic mine it went off harmlessly in your wake. It wasn't exactly correct, but nevertheless that was the idea. So we went off down the swept channel, down the coast of Northumberland, and the plan was that we would turn in towards the Tyne and steam at twenty-five knots up the channel so that any acoustic mines that had been dropped would go off in our wake.

I was actually officer of the watch, and I was told that I should wake the Captain when we passed the buoy before the one we were to turn round − the buoys were at five mile intervals, or were supposed to be, but in actual fact one of them had drifted. Well, I woke him when we passed the appropriate buoy, and we carried on for another fifteen minutes, or twenty minutes I think it was, and no buoy showed up so we carried on. We were scratching our heads, and thinking 'this is a bit odd', so we sent the navigator down to check that he'd got all the right things on the charts. A further twenty minutes passed, and finally another buoy turned up, so the destroyer in front of us, our leader − we were second in line − turned to starboard. So we followed, and went up what we thought was the swept channel. But it wasn't! And we hit the rocks rather hard, and fetched up on the rocks! To cut a long story short *Fame*, which was the ship leading us, was out of action for two years and we were out of action for a year, very badly damaged. We weren't going at full speed because it was about three o'clock in the morning – it was a very nasty night, with low visibility, very dark. We were only a cable or a cable and a half [*200 to 300 yards*] behind *Fame*, and I was keeping station on her wake, when suddenly there was this bang and she came back at us. I ordered hard to port and the Captain ordered full astern, and we just glanced off her and went on right alongside her.

Was there an enquiry about that?

I'll say! Oh yes, there was a Board of Enquiry. Unfortunately we went on just after high water on a spring tide. We couldn't get her off on the next tide; she wouldn't come off, despite tugs having a go. We lightened the ship, we got all the ammunition off over the rocks, we got the oil fuel over the rocks, so the Army who were helping us were all falling in the water, covered with fuel oil; you couldn't stand up properly – we were passing the ammunition over, one shell after another in a long chain of chaps.

I had to get the confidential books ashore up to Newcastle, so I borrowed a truck from the Army. My watchkeeping ticket was sitting in my cabin having been signed by the Captain, so I tucked it in my pocket, took it up and gave it to the Wren in the mail office at Newcastle and said this is a most important document, will you please makes sure it gets to the Admiralty as quickly as possible. And she did!

While it was unusual to find regular officers who had been promoted from the ranks, this process was certainly not unknown.

Doug Collier was one of those to bridge the considerable gulf between lower deck and wardroom.

I suppose the first effect of possible war came at the time of Munich. We were due to do a cruise down the west coast of South America in the *York*, down to Chile, and that was cancelled because, as the Captain told us over the tannoy, the international situation meant that the whole squadron would have to remain in the Atlantic, ready to move to the Med. That was really the first thought about war that impinged on me at all.

We came home to Chatham, the *York*'s home port, to pay off

in May 1939. By that time I had been designated a CW candidate – a possible candidate for commissioned rank – and so when I returned to Chatham I was sent to Chatham barracks and went on a school course. At the end of August, after the reserves had been called up and they had started bringing forward the commissioning of ships, I was drafted to a destroyer in the Home Fleet, HMS *Foxhound*. We travelled up by the Jellicoe Express, which used to leave Euston about five o'clock in the evening and arrive at Thurso about lunchtime the next day.[2] I did that two or three times over the next few years, and it was always a dreadful journey.

We went to sea the day I joined *Foxhound*, we did a patrol right up to the Denmark Strait, Iceland, Greenland and back again, and in fact we got back to Scapa on 3 September. *Foxhound* was one of three destroyers involved in the sinking of the first U-boat of the war – the *U.39* – on 14 September. That was one of the highlights. Most of the time it was very wet and uncomfortable and cold and boring! (laughs) Destroyers didn't generally go over the waves, they went through 'em!

Our time was spent patrolling with the Home Fleet, *Nelson* and *Rodney* and the old 'R' class battleships that were up there. We were in Scapa the night the *Royal Oak* was sunk, that was in October. After that the fleet moved its base down the west coast of Scotland to a place called Loch Ewe, which we visited on a couple of occasions when we were up there. The move was supposed to be all very secret, but in fact it wasn't because the Germans came and laid mines there, and the *Nelson* was mined leaving Loch Ewe for a patrol. Anyway, then Scapa was secured by putting down the blockships, and they started to build the causeways between the islands. My uncle, who during the war had an appointment on the staff of the Admiral commanding Orkneys and Shetlands, had a hand in building those. They were constructed with Italian POW labour.

Then came April 1940, when the Germans invaded Norway. *Foxhound* was one of the destroyers which took part in the Second Battle of Narvik on the 13th. We went up the fjord with

---

[2] A special train laid on for naval personnel reporting to the distant anchorage at Scapa Flow in the Orkneys. The name originated in the First World War, when the popular Admiral Sir John Jellicoe was in command of the fleet.

the *Warspite*, and finished up by sinking what was left of the ten German destroyers there – an absolute massacre. *Foxhound* actually went into Narvik harbour. I was one of 'A' gun's crew, and the German troops were on the jetty, and around, and we had a Lieutenant, J.J.S. Hooker, who was standing on the gun platform. Shot and shell flying everywhere, and he stood there and very deliberately – it was one of those vivid memories you have – took his .45 pistol and calmly and deliberately fired at some Germans along the jetty. We were hit by a certain amount of small arms fire and we had a few casualties from the action.

Then Italy came into the war and half our flotilla was sent down to Gibraltar to form part of what was known as Force H being set up there. We made a number of sorties into the Med. with Force H – Malta convoys. On another occasion we went up and bombarded Genoa – I don't quite know *why* we bombarded Genoa . . . (laughs) Personally during this time promotion became very rapid. By early 1940 I'd become an AB, then I passed the professional examination for Leading Seaman. We did a couple of trips down the west coast of Africa, down to Walfish Bay, and I passed for PO on one visit to Freetown, early in 1941. In July 1941 I was promoted to Acting PO, which made me surplus to the ship's requirements, and I was sent back to the UK where I went to gunnery school. I qualified as a gunnery control rating, in which you either sat in the director control tower and directed gunfire by spotting from there, or operated the fire control equipment in what was known as the transmitting station. That was from July until December 1941, when I was drafted to the cruiser *Liverpool* which was finishing a refit at Govan, on the Clyde.

Liverpool had been torpedoed during the Crete campaign and her whole bow section blown off. She'd been patched up at Alexandria and then gone across the Pacific to San Francisco and gone into the US Navy Yard at Mare Island for a complete new bow. I joined the ship in December and we sailed in the New Year to join the Home Fleet again. Soon after I'd joined, my divisional officer sent for me and said the Captain wished to see me. So I went along to see the Captain, and he said 'I understand you're a CW candidate?' I said 'I believe that's so, sir.' He said 'Well, I have to advise you that I don't approve of promotion to commissioned rank from the lower deck, so I'm being quite straightforward with you, I'm going to destroy your CW form. I've no doubt you'll make a good Warrant Officer.' Utterly frank. It was the only occasion in the whole of my career that this prejudice was openly expressed. So that was that.

Luckily the Captain of his next ship held a more liberal view.

In September 1942 I went to a new destroyer, HMS *Obedient*, which was then building at Denny's yard on the Clyde at Dumbarton. We commissioned her the following month – the ship's company arrived from Chatham by train and marched on board, which was the custom, then the lower deck was cleared and the skipper, Lieutenant Commander Kinloch, addressed us. He said something like. 'We're commissioning today and we shall be joining the Home Fleet, and we've got a lot of hard work to do working up.' He said 'you see that I've got two and a half stripes on my cuff, and that's the height of my ambition – I really want to be a farmer.' He said 'I've got a plain peak to my cap – I don't wish anything more because it gets heavy, and by the way, I think it's Trafalgar Day today but don't get worried about it because it's nothing to do with us!'

What did you make of that?

Well, it was something unusual. He was a brilliant Captain, first class. But his ambition was to be a farmer – he used to read farming magazines up on the bridge. We were on Russian convoys, and on 31 December 1942 we were escorting a convoy off the North Cape in company with a number of other ships of our flotilla, when we ran into the *Lützow* and *Admiral Hipper* and some German destroyers. We were quite involved in that, for which Kinloch got promoted to Commander and got a DSO. That was a pretty fierce action.

After I joined the *Obedient*, Kinloch discovered that I had been a CW candidate and asked what happened and why. When I told him he said that didn't seem entirely fair, and he restarted my application. In consequence of that, in August 1943 I went before a preselection board for commissioned rank, which recommended me, and I left the ship almost immediately for HMS *Collingwood*, Fareham. You did an eight-month course there which covered all that was considered necessary, and you got a number of certificates at the end of it.

Despite the exigencies of war, the Navy continued to place a heavy emphasis on social skills as well as the more obviously professional ones such as seamanship.

They knew you'd have to remember which knife and fork to use! During the eight months you moved progressively into the wardroom social side. You had mess guest nights, and you had small receptions and cocktail parties, where you practised small talk and that sort of thing. The transition was made subtly. At the end of it I was commissioned as an Acting Sub-Lieutenant, on 1 May 1944.

Was your commission a temporary one, like those for people who had joined during wartime?

No, if you were a candidate for commissioned rank as a regular rating, then you did exactly the same training as pre-war, and you were promoted as a permanent officer. The Navy right through the war kept the advancement of its regular ratings and regular officers exactly as it had been pre-war, and quite separate from all the rest.

As a newly-promoted Sub-Lieutenant I did four months of technical courses, and then in September I was appointed to my first ship as an officer – another destroyer, the *Active*. We operated in the Channel up until just after Christmas, when we were moved to the Aegean. There were all sorts of odd people steaming round the Aegean at that time, like the Eastern Med. Raiding Forces – cloak and dagger chaps. One I particularly recall was a Scandinavian who wore the uniform of a Major in a Guards regiment – he came on board one day and asked if we were going anywhere in the vicinity of Rhodes for any reason. The answer was yes, so he said 'Well, can you take me with you?' He said 'There's a Hetman so-and-so who is making a nuisance of himself, and I think I must go and cut his throat.' We dropped him off the coast in a little dinghy, and away he went. When we were back in Simi some short time later we met up with him again, and I said 'Did you find your Hetman and cut his throat?' And he said 'Yes, I found him in bed with his mistress! Cut both their throats!' Some of the raiding troops we took around with us were the Greek Sacred Heart Regiment – you were never quite sure who *they* were out to get!

Anyway, after VE Day we took the surrender of Rhodes. We got mixed up in the battle between the Greek government and the Communists, and that was a fascinating affair. We used to go round the Greek islands, up to Samos and Chios, and Mytilene, just keeping in touch. So we would go into one of these islands, where we would find the blue and white government flag, and we used to do things naval fashion – we'd have a little party and invite people on board, the mayor and people like that. Then perhaps a month later we'd go back, and the red flag would be flying, so to avoid taking sides we'd entertain the mayor and so on again – and the same people would come back on board!

So the European war finished and we were sent back to Gibraltar, where we formed part of an air sea rescue patrol. There were American aircraft ferrying troops back to the States, and there was an air sea rescue patrol set up across the Atlantic – we used to go out on seven day patrols.

I'd been promoted to Lieutenant, and it was decided I was surplus to requirements – for that sort of rank we had too many officers – so I was shipped home from Gib. Which got me my first command! There was a flotilla of landing craft coming back from the Mediterranean, and they were to be escorted by some armed trawlers. Well, the landing craft were all commanded by Sub-Lieutenants, RNVR, and the trawlers were all commanded by Skippers, RNR, so it was decided there ought to be a regular RN officer in charge somewhere and I was appointed to become 'Admiral' of this lot. I think there were about eight or ten landing craft and four trawlers. So we set off from Gibraltar. I left all the technical stuff to the Skipper of the trawler I was on – I'd say where are we? And he'd point the stem of his pipe at the chart. In fact he used the stem of his pipe for most of his navigation. Anyway, we got off Corunna, and the weather forecast we got was pretty bad for the Bay, so I took a big executive decision and we put into El Ferrol for a couple of days. It seemed to be the best place to go. We stayed there for a couple of days and then got back to Plymouth, where I handed over my command. I was then twenty-three.

I then reported to the Naval Assistant to the Second Sea Lord – that's the department which dealt with officers' appointments, located in Queen Anne's Mansions. I found the splendid elderly Commander who did the Lieutenants' appointments and I bowled up there and said 'Sir, what have you got for me?' 'Oh well, we're commissioning some big destroyers now for the Far East – I'll fit you in as a second or third hand.' I said 'Sir, I've just been First Lieutenant.' He said I could still be fitted in as second or third hand – and then a gleam came into his eye – unless I'd like to fly? He said 'Now, there's a future for a young man like you; we want more regular officers in the FAA, and we could get you off to Canada for a quick pilot's course, six months, back, do some operational flying training, and then out to the Pacific – that's where the war's going to be. And as to the future, you could have your own squadron in fifteen, eighteen months.' And I suppose I took it all hook, line and sinker; so I was persuaded to go off and be an aviator.

What they had done was they had gathered together about sixty Lieutenants of my age and seniority and they pushed them through flying training because the Fleet Air Arm by that time was something like ninety-five per cent RNVR and five per cent permanent officers, and they wanted to even up the imbalance.

Then suddenly came VJ Day. Now all these naval aviation trainees, the routine ones, had gone to the States and Canada to do their flying training, under the Commonwealth Air Training Scheme. Immediately VJ Day passed that chopped just like that. Some of these young lads said they'd been airborne, doing a training trip, and they'd landed to be told get fell in over there – you're on your way back to the UK! It stopped just like that.

And we in fact were hauled in to help sort out these lads who were arriving back in droves. They came back on the *Queen Elizabeth* and the *Queen Mary*. Obviously we knew we wouldn't now be going to Canada or the States for our flying training, but they'd yet to decide what to do with us.

Then we were told that we would continue our flying training with the RAF at a little grass field in Wiltshire. Somebody looked on a map and couldn't even find it! So we went off there and we did our elementary flying training in Tiger Moths. It was a rather disjointed training because they'd started de-mobilizing, so you'd have a flying instructor who'd do a couple of trips with you, and then you'd see him one morning and he'd say 'I'm handing you over to Flight Lieutenant so-and-so, I'm off to be demobbed.' It really was chaotic. But I do recall my initial flying instructor. He was a one-eyed Warrant Officer – WO Horsham – or as he introduced himself (slips into Cockney) accent 'The naime's 'Orsham, sir, Warrant Officer 'Orsham – "Straight 'n level Charlie" they calls me. All them other buggers from me course'r dead!'

Anyway, I got a good grounding from WO Horsham. That went on I think for about three months, in the spring of 1946; the progression was EFT then to service flying training, then you went on operational flying training. When we finished our EFT, somebody said 'Well, where do we go now?' And the reply was 'We don't know – we'll have to find somewhere', and we were sent on leave. Which was fine – we hadn't had much leave at all. Then I got a telegram out of the blue telling me to report to another RAF station, this time in Northumberland. This was a base that had been used by the Free French during the war – it had a hell of a reputation in Newcastle! We carried out our service flying training there on Harvards. The RAF people were still being demobbed the whole time, and conti-nuity was practically non-existent. We finished there towards the end of 1946, and then went to the Royal Naval Air Station at Lossiemouth up in Morayshire, which the Navy had moved into some three months previously, for our operational flying training. We moved around the country doing various things, and eventually I got to an operational squadron for the first time in October 1947. So much for the command of a squadron in fifteen months!

3

MERCHANT SERVICE

At the outbreak of war the British Merchant Navy was still the largest mercantile marine in the world, dwarfing even that of the United States. It included an enormous variety of ships, from huge luxury liners to the tankers of the big oil companies, and the 'rust-buckets' that plied the coastal trade or tramped to and fro in the remotest parts of the globe. These ships and men carried Britain's huge foreign trade to its destinations and brought food and raw materials from most of the countries of the world to the British Isles.

For many young men in the 1920s and 30s, going to sea was the only way they could travel and see the world; many others simply sought escape from the poverty and restrictions of provincial life.

When the war started the convoy system was reintroduced, as the Germans set out to starve Britain into defeat by sinking the shipping that brought her supplies. The Merchant Navy found itself pitched into the front line, and suffered terrible losses. At least 45,000 British merchant seamen had been listed as killed, wounded or missing by 1945, and millions of tons of shipping, equipment, food and raw materials had been sent to the bottom of the sea. A war was fought which was as vital to victory as the RAF's achievement in the Battle of Britain, or the Army's in assisting in the liberation of Europe in 1944–45.

The Merchant Service secured many of its sailors from the port and dock areas of the country, boys and young men who were caught by the romance of the sea, and the excitement of a travelling life. *Leslie Beavan* was born and brought up at Woolwich in South London, 'a kid right on top of the docks'.

It was a hive of industry in them days. Ships everywhere. So much adventure down there. I used to spend all my time watching these big P. & O. boats and thinking where they were going to. Next port – where? You dreamed of it. At fourteen I just mentioned casually to a friend that I'd like to go to sea, and he said 'My sister's engaged to a bloke on the ships – I'll have a word with him.' The very next night I had the superintendent of the catering department of the New Zealand Shipping Company at my door, asking my mother would I like to go to sea. That was 1937.

I thought it was difficult to get into the Merchant Navy?

Not in them days. They were short of boys. I went down the shipping company, signed on next day and I was away. That's how easy it was in 1937. There were kids younger than me. But whether you started at fourteen or twenty-four, your first jobs were always the boys' jobs. No matter who you was. And that's how you went on. I've my discharge book here, and my first voyage was to New Zealand, for meat.

I notice they always stamp your book after a voyage.

You only got two stamps in the Merchant Navy – Very Good, or DR for declined to report. If you done your job properly you got Very Good, Very Good [the book has two assessment columns, 'For ability' and 'For general conduct']. Thank the Lord I got that all the way through, but if you had trouble with the Skipper, or you went absent or you didn't do your job properly you got DR, DR. And once you got that in your book you'd have a job getting another ship.

Once you joined a ship you were there, you lived on that ship. At night time they turned the electricity and power off to save money, that's how bad they were. In port in depth of winter you froze to death but you couldn't do anything about it, that was all they had. Cabins were never locked up, but nothing was ever stolen. I didn't hear in all them years one man pinching off anybody else. Even fags. You used to buy your fags by the thousand and you always used to find a packet of fags open on the top there with fifty in it, and nobody thought about taking them.

I started off as a steward's boy. On my first ship I looked after the engineers – they called me an engineers' mess room boy. You had to clean their cabins, look after their mess and their food, and that lark. They were all right. Of course on that ship I was the baby!

We went to Swansea, then Newport, then out to New Zealand via the Panama Canal. Wonderful country. Beautiful. I would have loved to have stayed out there. In fact on that ship there was another young lad, a little Jewish boy called Aubrey, who I shared a cabin with. He said to me when we got to New Zealand he was just leaving, going ashore. A lot of them did in those days – went ashore and started life again. I didn't believe it, but one night I came back aboard and he'd taken his little couple of carrier bags of clothing and he'd gone – jumped ship. He might be Prime Minister of New Zealand by now!

But New Zealand was wonderful in them days, because it was still like – primitive. The docks and harbours were all lovely clean water, fish everywhere, and full of hulks of old sailing boats. I remember being at Auckland and seeing the Pan Am clippers coming in.

After a few voyages I went from the New Zealand Shipping Company to the Port Line. It was the same as the NZSC, doing the same job; going down to the Argentine for beef during the war. We went down there just after the *Graf Spee* incident, and as you went into the River Plate you could see the remains of the *Graf Spee* just outside, lying in shallow water. All the superstructure, rusting away.

That was a nice place to go, Buenos Aires, but they were pro-German. You had to be very careful.

You might get beaten up?

Well, I never saw anyone get beaten up, but I think they could have learned information. Then again I don't suppose they were lost for information down there, because ships were coming and going all the time.

Another place like that was Spain. I went there in a teeny Cardiff collier called the *Ogmore Castle*. She shouldn't have been a deep sea boat at all, but during the war anything that floated they bunged here there and everywhere, so we went to Spain with a cargo of coal. They were very short of escorts, the Royal Navy. They'd send out fifty ships and two corvettes, and a merchant ship with a catapulted aircraft on it which never got used.

Once it took off it couldn't get back again. That's all we had in them days. But we went to Spain and dropped the coal, which at the time they said was going straight to Germany! They used to bung all these old guns on the ships – I think to give you confidence, because you never used them. A submarine didn't tell you he was coming, he just hit you first. So you didn't get a chance to fire back at them. Anyway, we had these four or five gunners, and when we went to a place like Spain they had to dismantle everything – the gunners used to take all the armaments and stow 'em away where they wouldn't be seen – and they used to change into civvies. When we came out of there, I'm sure the Spaniards were telling the Germans everything that went on.

I can remember being in Gibraltar the time the *Ark Royal* was sunk. There were thousands of matelots queuing up to get in the Post Office to send telegrams home to their wives and mothers that they're safe. We had about a month there before they ventured out, and we had a few corvettes and an escort carrier called the *Audacity*. She was only an ordinary converted merchant ship.

This was a slow old convoy – we could only do seven knots – and German aircraft were coming up there so they could tell a sub to go out and meet you at night time. So at night, the middle of the night, bang, bang, bang, ships are getting blown up left right and centre. They couldn't miss, could they?

Well this Commander Walker, RN,[3] who died just at the end of the war funnily enough – he done so much to win that war, I don't think he's ever been recognized – about four or five nights out he said that at a certain time, on a given signal, he wanted star shells put up. Remember there was total blackout all the time, you couldn't light a fag or nothing. Suddenly in the middle of the night the whole area is like daylight – every ship put star shells up, and they could see these bloody submarines, they could see them lying there. They couldn't

[3] Commander, later Captain, F.J. 'Johnnie' Walker, senior officer of the 36th Escort Group and then the famous 2nd Support Group.

hang about, they had to dive, with our corvettes after 'em.

But even that didn't stop us getting attacked. Nobody stopped for survivors, but every large ship in the convoy had a load of roping like, netting, and if the men got near enough to grab hold of that netting you'd save 'em. But you weren't allowed to stop. It's like what happened to us. Remember, we had copper ore in every hold, all heavy stuff, and as a rule once you got hit, that's it, you're down like a stone, wallop. They've got no chance, down in about a minute, gone.

We never took our life-jackets off the whole trip, we was always in our clothes ready to jump overboard. We saw them going day after day, even the escorts – the escort carrier was blown up, and that carried a lot of survivors on it; as they could get hold of 'em they put them on there. Anyway, this night there was a big explosion. I didn't know what it was, all I knew was the red light's gone on on the bridge which means abandon ship, and they're putting down these old boats. I was what, eighteen then – and I can always hear like even today a voice saying 'Jump Les! Jump Les!' I jumped in this boat and we rowed around in the Atlantic there – Bay of Biscay somewhere. Thank God it was a good night. It wasn't rough, it wasn't cold, and the ship just sort of nosed down a bit. Three or four hours later they decided to go back aboard her. And we did, we went back aboard. The convoy had gone, and it took about three or four hours and a lot of frantic action to get going again, but we made it back to discharge our cargo and then pay off.

And if you hadn't been able to reboard the ship?

I don't know what we'd have done, to tell you the truth! I don't know. I suppose we'd have rowed round till we got sighted or picked up. If we'd got stuck there God knows what might have happened. We had no provisions, and of course we were in the Bay of Biscay. It might have been our lot, anyway. It might have been rough the next day, and that would've been it. I don't know. You never had no thoughts of these things. And you never felt scared – with all that going on, you never felt scared. I don't know why.

Subsequent trips on a new ship were just as eventful.

The first time out on the *Port Melbourne* I went back to South America, Buenos Aires. The only excitement was coming home we found an empty lifeboat in the middle of the Atlantic. And the funny thing about that was you had to be so careful, 'cos sometimes they'd leave decoys – they used to leave a decoy there so you stopped, and wallop, the submarine's been waiting for you to stop! We spotted this lifeboat floating about, and you're trying to see if you can save anybody, and the way the Captain had to do it was round and round it like that, getting nearer and nearer, but there was nothing in it. They sank it, if I remember rightly, got rid of it, otherwise other ships might have been caught.

Next trip was to Australia and New Zealand, then we went to Beira, Lourenço Marques, Durban, Cape Town, and then back to South America and that, picked up meat and brought it home again. On that trip we had the first attack with glider bombs. The Germans started using these radio controlled bombs, so as you got off the coast of Spain again, up near home, their planes would come out and release a flying bomb, and they would direct it to any ship. The ship would alter course and the bomb would alter course as well. It would follow the ship it was after. They were very clever, them Germans. So the orders were to shoot this glider bomb. You couldn't hit the plane up there keeping it radio controlled.

The only thing about it was it didn't sink ships, it blew the top off them – did a lot of damage and probably killed all the people up there. We were getting attacked periodically by these guided bombs, and they were wrecking ship after ship. Eventually it was our turn to be the biggest ship left – they were going for the biggest ones.

I can always remember this Sunday afternoon, going right down in the bowels of the ship to get something, and it suddenly started. The first you knew was the ack-ack going up, bang-bang-bang, every ship was opening up, trying to get these bombs, and I'm down there. The sound was magnified, and I'm thinking that the other side of this bulkhead was all our ammunition! And I couldn't climb up them ladders again, me legs were like rubber. That was the first time I'd really had it, you know. I was stuck down there.

When I got back up they told me this glider bomb had missed us by feet. It had just hit the water by the side of us.

I've had so much luck in wartime. I missed two ships that I would have been blown to bits on. The first one was when I was sent up to Liverpool to join the *Port Hunter*, and she's chock-a-block with ammunition, tanks and everything else, all ready to go to the Far East, and he said 'Sorry, you're job's been taken, you've got to wait here for the next one' – which was the old *Port Melbourne* coming in. So I waited, and two weeks later I went out on the *Melbourne* which had the same cargo. The *Port Hunter* left a fortnight ahead of us, same course through the Panama Canal to Australia, and just before she got to Panama she took a torpedo. Blew her to bits. And I'd have been on that one, it was only pure luck that somebody had taken the job instead of me. The second one was when two of my mates said to me 'We're sailing for Algiers next week, we've got a job for you on the ship. Come and join us.' As I'd just come back so had money in my pocket, I said 'Wait till I've spent my bloody money – I'm going to have my leave first!' And the ship went out and got blown apart off Algiers – I think she was blown in half, and the rear part, where all the accommodation was, went down like a lift.

Were your family aware how dangerous it was?

Well, my dad wanted to stop me going but he couldn't. I also had a brother as a gunner in the Merchant Navy – he was an RN gunner, and they sent him on merchant ships. Everybody survived, thank God.

His last ship during the war was the *Queen Elizabeth*, which he joined at Gourock on the Clyde. 1,030 feet long and with a beam of 118½ feet, the giant Cunarder was bigger than the Navy's battleships.

She had her own newspaper, football pools, own bulletins, and she had three cinemas, her own Pig & Whistle, like a real pub. And in New York they treated us like heroes. We were bringing over 15,000 American troops every trip and taking back 3,000 wounded, backwards and forwards.

Were you ever attacked?

Not on the big 'uns. The surprising thing about the Queens

was they never had any antisubmarine escort. But they were
doing thirty knots. We never had an attack on them ships.
Never had a warning or anything. They were zig-zagging all the
time. When you'd got all them dinners, there might be piles of
plates in the mess rooms to be washed, or just been washed.
The ship'd take a zig-zag and the lot'd go – you'd hear clattering – all these plates going on the deck! Cunard must have lost
thousands of plates every trip. I've often said that if the Atlantic
Ocean dried up, I could walk from Southampton to New York
following Cunard plates!

The Americans looked after the food and everything else,
they really looked after their boys, looked after 'em one
hundred per cent. They had masses of ice cream, masses of
fresh fruit, tinned fruit. When we took the injured back to New
York, they were met well out in the bay by floating bands, all
these women, Army people and that, they were given such a
welcome. And when I think how our boys came back to
nothing. They slipped into Glasgow or Liverpool and nobody
ever knew they came back.

How did you get on with the Americans?

Oh, lovely people, yeah. We had wonderful times in America.
They looked after service people, and we were classed as servicemen. I could go out in New York, every night to a different
function. I could go and see the top stars in them days, Louis
Armstrong, Bing Crosby. You could go anywhere in New York
– you was a guest of the town. It was fantastic, it really was. I
even worked in New York. We used to have our repairs there,
so you might be there three weeks. To earn a few bob I worked
at Bloomingdales as a packer. I suppose I got a couple of
dollars a day; it helped your money out.

Were you tempted to stay there?

No, I never wanted to stay there. I liked it – nice to visit. But
I wouldn't have liked to stay there.

Why not?

Well, it's the bustle of the place, hustle and bustle – though
New York isn't true of America. I went to Virginia, Georgia,
Pennsylvania and found them different again.

The path to becoming a Merchant Navy officer usually started with the young hopeful joining as an apprentice, as *Harry Bird* did in 1937.

We were a family of limited means, so Dartmouth college, Pangbourne and *Worcester* were all out of the question, as were the major shipping lines who required large premiums from cadets. However, in my father's bank, Coutts & Co., a colleague had a nephew who was an apprentice in the Bank Line – Andrew Weir & Company. My father followed up this lead, and in due course we attended for interview at the London office of this Glasgow firm.

We were interviewed by a Scottish Marine Superintendent, Captain Howie, who made a point of taking me aside to ask if it was indeed my choice to go to sea, to which I replied yes. Following a medical examination and a Board of Trade eyesight test my indentures were prepared, duly signed, witnessed and registered, and I was bound apprentice to my master, Andrew Weir & Co. Points of interest in the indentures included, as I recall, 'Apprentice not to frequent Taverns and Alehouses unless upon his master's business' and 'Master to provide apprentice with sufficient meat, drink, lodging, etc.' though Board of Trade scales of provisions were very meagre at this time – one tin of condensed milk was the issue for three weeks! My pay was £4 for the first year, £6 for the second, £8 for the third and £12 for the final year, plus a £10 annual bonus for good conduct. From this deductions were made for health insurance and unemployment insurance.

Prior to joining your first ship, the company sent a list to your parents or guardians detailing the necessary clothes and things to be taken to sea. This list included three books, Nicholl's *Guide to the Board of Trade Examinations Vol.1*, Nicholl's *Seamanship*, and Norie's *Nautical Tables*.

Nicholl's *Guide* was an extremely well written textbook, starting from basic arithmetic, geometry and algebra and proceeding through spherical trigonometry to celestial navigation. I left school with a school certificate in mathematics, and was able to teach myself spherical trig and celestial navigation from the *Guide*.

The company registered each of its apprentices with the

Merchant Navy Training Board, from whom the apprentice received a syllabus of study indicating what subjects should be studied during each of the four years of the apprenticeship, there being a written examination at the end of each year, which was held on board under supervision.

The syllabus covered seamanship, navigation, ship construction, cargo work and engineering. I can recall that on very hot nights when I couldn't sleep, I would slip out of the cabin I shared with two others, squeeze a cup of lukewarm tea out of the pot in the engineers' mess room – no milk of course – and read my books for an hour or so.

In the four ships of my apprenticeship, I was very fortunate to serve under Masters and officers willing to share their skills and help with any problems in the book work.

None of them viewed you as a threat?

No, I never felt the officers teaching me were apprehensive about me taking their jobs. They were already on the ladder of promotion, and it was unlikely that I could overtake them.

The practical side of their instruction was seamanship, which in most cases started with the apprentice learning to steer the ship. In my case, in addition to my eight hours deck work I had to report to the bridge during the Chief Officer's dog watch and under his eye, and that of the helmsman, take the wheel and learn how to steer for an hour. Also I had to learn how to box the compass in quarter points. This drill continued until the Chief Officer was satisfied that I was competent to steer.

Our Master would examine us apprentices every Sunday morning when at sea on the thirty-one International Regulations for the Prevention of Collisions at Sea, which had to be learnt by heart; on the buoyage system, flags and other general items. Officers would teach you to recognize the stars, how to take land bearings, how to take bearings of heavenly bodies and calculate the error of the compass, how to work out the noon latitude from a sextant sight of the sun, or the ship's position from star observations; or question you about the ship's construction to make sure you kept your eyes open as you worked about the decks or in the holds.

Our lodging was a small cabin for three, of which only two could dress at the same time! Although it had two portholes it was very hot in the tropics and we had no fan, so used to sleep on deck. There was no proper wash place for apprentices, but we were occasionally allowed to take a bucket bath in the officers' bathroom. Otherwise we washed on deck.

The basic working week for deckhands and apprentices was sixty-four hours, in two four-hour watches per day plus a further eight hours worked during the week, usually as four two-hour periods. Deckhands were eligible for overtime payments, but these were avoided like the plague by shipowners, and we apprentices were invariably called out to do the extra work as we weren't eligible for overtime! On two occasions I collapsed from physical exhaustion, and once fell asleep at the wheel. On collapsing, you were simply dosed with rum and put in your bunk to recover. During a four-hour day watch, you would do one or two hours at the wheel and the rest of the time on deck work. At night you would steer for one or two hours then take over as lookout on the forecastle head or stand by to run messages for the officer of the watch. Apprentices' work included polishing brass; cleaning the windows; holystoning and scrubbing the decks; washing paintwork on deck and in the accommodation; chipping rust; repainting; cleaning holds and bilges between cargoes; preparing the holds for special cargoes like grain, gunny bales or phosphates; overhauling standing and running rigging; wire and rope splicing; repairing tarpaulin hatch covers; maintaining lifeboats, firefighting equipment and so on; and catching rats.

In port, the apprentices would be engaged in tallying cargo in and out of the holds, acting as watchman in the holds to prevent the dockers stealing and damaging cargo, working over the side chipping off rust and repainting the hull, repainting draught and load lines, working as night watchman on the gangway, and so forth.

Another skill required of the Bank Line's prospective officers was that they pick up Indian dialects, since large numbers of Indian crewmen were employed.

Bank Line ships traded frequently out of Calcutta, which we called our home port out there, and sailed largely in hot climates for which the Indian seamen were more suited. Furthermore, with ships in the 5,000 tons gross class, a larger Indian crew than a white crew for a ship of comparable size would be carried.

The method of recruiting these Indian crews was rather interesting. The Marine Superintendent in Calcutta would let it be known on the grapevine that a crew would be required for a certain vessel on a particular date. Serangs [bosuns] would appear at the office and offer their services in providing a crew. The Marine Superintendent would charge the Serang of his choice with producing the crew, deck or engine room as required; the Serangs would then return to their villages and recruit their family and friends, so the crew had a unity right from the start.

In 1941, after the successful completion of his four years as an apprentice, he sat and passed a professional examination. This allowed him to apply for jobs as a Third Officer.

On passing the exam in London, I accepted a post offered to me as a Third Mate in the Anglo-Saxon Petroleum Company, and was instructed to join the MV *Mactra* at Shellhaven, on the Thames.

Why did you opt for tanker duty, which was known to be more dangerous?

I think my main reason was that during my time as an apprentice in cargo ships I'd observed that although the Chief Officer was held responsible for the safe and proper loading and discharging of cargo, he really had little control over these operations, and was very much in the hands of stevedores and dockers – and this situation didn't suit my nature. I like to make my own mistakes and accept the responsibility for them. In tankers, the officer on deck has the complete loading or discharging operation in his control.

My first watch on the *Mactra* was a deck watch, ballasting the ship. It was all very strange, as I had no practical experience of tankers, but with the guidance of the Chief Officer, the senior apprentice and the Chinese pumpman my tanker education commenced!

The *Mactra* was a tanker of 9,000 tons deadweight, divided into nine main tank sections, each one of which was again divided into three, thus making twenty-seven tanks in all. She had two pump rooms, one forward and one aft, a ring main and some sixty-five valves controlling the flow of oil.

We sailed from the Thames soon after, and joined a coastal convoy sailing north under cover of darkness. We were under threat from E-boats and aircraft as well as the problem of navigating in darkness through the narrow swept channel, so you can imagine my dismay, on this my first bridge watch as a new Third Officer on a strange ship, to find that the Master, who was on the bridge, was plainly under the influence and of no practical help.

Was drinking at sea commonplace?

I'm afraid alcohol was a bit of an occupational hazard where the seafarer was concerned. I've seen it destroy the livelihood and careers of several men, both seamen and officers – including Masters. However, I managed to survive the four-hour watch without hitting the stern of the vessel ahead, and without getting swept out of the channel by the tide. Thankfully the ship ahead which I was following was a good navigator, because I learned later that in coastal convoys you must carefully check off the buoys yourself. In one convoy six ships ran aground one night because they were following a leader who led them astray!

Proceeding through the Pentland Firth, we ended up at Loch Ewe on the west coast of Scotland, which was an assembly point for transatlantic convoys. Up to seventy or so ships would be organized here for an ocean crossing. Prior to sailing, a Masters' conference would be called by the Convoy Commodore [*usually a retired RN officer*]. The Master and a radio officer or navigating officer from each ship would attend the meeting, where the Commodore would outline his proposed route, details of special signals and action in case of attack by air or sea. Sometimes the senior officer of the Naval escort would also be present.

At this particular time in the war we were convoyed to a point in mid-Atlantic and then proceeded independently to our destinations. In our case we were bound for Curaçao in the

Caribbean to load oil for the UK. Approaching the Mona Passage, one of the entrances into the Caribbean, we were advised by radio from the Admiralty that a U-boat was waiting for us there, so we diverted our course and entered the Caribbean through the Sombrero Passage and reached Curaçao safely. After loading we proceeded to Halifax, Nova Scotia and there joined a transatlantic convoy home.

Our next voyage to Curaçao followed similar lines with the added complications that the Master was removed from the ship in Loch Ewe with DT's and the Second Officer with a nervous breakdown as a result of previous experiences. This meant that the former Chief Officer became Master and I became Second Officer. Together we worked the ship to Curaçao and back, standing watch and watch about in convoy and violent North Atlantic weather.

On our third trip we loaded at Curaçao and then sailed independently to Cape Town, where the Second Radio Officer and I took the cable car up to the top of Table Mountain one afternoon. Back in the city, we decided to buy a second-hand gramophone for the ship. This we managed, but we could only get one record in the second-hand shop and all the other shops were closed by then. It was a Deanna Durbin record, one side of which was the 'Maids of Cadiz'. That record was played endlessly from Cape Town to Abadan, our next loading port.

In those days the Persian Gulf had only three lighthouses from the Strait of Hormuz to the pilot station at the mouth of the Shatt-al-Arab. My admiration for our new Master, Captain McDougall, who took us up and down the Gulf with no lights or navigational aids, is unbounding.

Sailing without lights as we did, I have every reason to believe that I ran down a dhow one night, also sailing without lights, but in wartime you didn't stop to enquire.

Arriving back at Abadan after one of our Indian Ocean delivery runs, we found we had orders to load for Port Said. From Port Said we went to Haifa, and became one of three tankers – *Mactra, Macoma* and *San Venancio* – involved in fuelling the fleet. We would load in Haifa, sail together in our own special convoy, one drop off at Port Said, another or perhaps both at Alexandria, and later we went to Malta. Our visit to Malta was quite revealing – the bomb damage was frightful. We went to the cinema, a former theatre, and sat in one of the boxes overlooking the stage. There were no chairs, we sat on orange boxes. In Alexandria we would lie at anchor in the harbour, with destroyers and corvettes coming alongside for fuel. In the case of battleships and such large vessels, we would go alongside them.

On one of our trips from Haifa to Alexandria we found a sister ship, *Delphinula*, aground on a pinnacle just outside Alex. She was carrying petrol, which was leaking out of the hull. A tug approached her, accidentally ignited the vapour, the ship blew up and burned for three weeks, shooting up a thick black cloud which could be seen from miles away. Incidentally, in the ship at the time was an apprentice, Peter Adlam, enjoying a siesta at the time of the explosion. He was picked up and in later life became Chief Officer of Shell's first oil drilling ship, and Captain Superintendent of the Gravesend Sea School. If you should visit the Merchant Navy memorial on Tower Hill, on each side of the horseshoe you will see a figure, one a seaman in his duffle coat, the other a junior officer in his bridge coat. Peter Adlam was the model for the figure of the junior officer.

On 17 January 1944, two years and eleven days since leaving England, I was paid off the *Mactra* in Port Said and put in the British hospital, suffering from jaundice and malaria and in a very bad way. Somehow I lost the first twenty-four hours in hospital, but surfaced to find that I was sharing a room with a young purser from a Dutch liner. Later the purser was replaced by a British Third Officer, like myself, by the name of Frank Packman.

The doctor in charge, the matron and sisters were British and the rest of the staff were Egyptian. The British hospital normally dealt with the British residents and merchant seamen, but during the war took in Army wives and Wrens. Some of the wives were pregnant, and an Irish sister ran a book among the staff and patients as to the time of arrival and sex of the imminent offspring. On one occasion the matron asked Frank and me to support the young parents at the baptism in the hospital chapel.

When I had recovered, the matron said that really she should ask my company's agent to arrange accommodation for me in a hotel until a passage could be arranged for me to get to the UK – such passages being very few and far between. However, the matron said that if I would work with her I could stay in my room in the hospital, and this I chose to do.

She approached me one day saying that she had a number of Wrens in the hospital who wished to go shopping in the town. She couldn't let them go into town on their own and wished me to escort them in small numbers on shopping trips, all of which was good fun. Another job she put my way was to assist the padre of the Mission to Seamen by taking the Mission launch and visiting the ships in the port with books and magazines, and broadcasting the existence and whereabouts of the Mission. On another occasion I was engaged in taking the launch, collecting apprentices from various ships, taking them to the cinema, then to the Mission for tea and back to their ships.

Eventually a passage became available on the troopship *Cameronia*, where I found some forty MN personnel in a dormitory on board. It was a boring voyage, and I was glad to see Liverpool and then home.

In contrast to the officers, who were permanent employees of their company, the men were simply signed on at a Shipping Federation office prior to each voyage. Between ships they were effectively unemployed, but it was a system which merchant seamen like *Sydney Hall* knew and liked, largely because of the freedom it gave them.

We sailed from Liverpool about the beginning of March 1941, bound for the Hudson River and New Jersey. The crossing in convoy was uneventful and we sailed into the Hudson and past Staten Island to the town of Bayonne on the Jersey River. It was very interesting on entering the dock to see some six or seven men on the far side who were catcalling and doing the Nazi salute to us. Someone in the gun crew trained the gun round towards them, and it was amusing to see them rush off to another appointment!

Ships were being equipped with guns for defence against U-boats and aircraft. The guns were 1914 vintage, and mounted on reinforced platforms on the stern. A bit later in the war some ships got more modern guns such as Bofors. Initially the guns were crewed by an RN rating, usually a PO, and the other members of the team came from the ship's crew.

When loading was completed the ship pulled out into the Hudson to await other ships moving up to Canada. The last boat back to the ship from shore was at eleven p.m., and one evening three of us missed it. We had to stretch out on some park benches near the waterfront in Bayonne. I was fast asleep in the early hours and was awakened by someone hitting the soles of my feet – it was a policeman using his truncheon. When told why we were on the benches he said 'Too bad' and advised us to take a walk around the block. We did, got down on the same benches and slept for the rest of the night.

After a couple of days we sailed north to St John's, Newfoundland to await a convoy to the UK. We joined up with other ships out of Halifax to make quite a big convoy, and I recall being surprised at the strength of the escort; probably some VIP or some special cargo on one of the ships. I think this was the first time we had had air cover from Catalinas for a good part of the voyage. All the same we were subjected to attack twice. On both occasions the escort seemed to have the upper hand quickly and there was a lot of depth charging. I think three of the ships were sunk. We lost one of our seamen overboard on that trip – he was in the lifeboat repairing some storm damage when a big sea swamped the boat and washed him overboard. The ship circled, but there was a bad squall and we never found him.

We got back to Liverpool about the end of April and I signed off. About this time, I think it was, that seamen came under the Board of Trade administration. All seamen were formed into pools based at the various ports in the UK. A seaman could choose his own pool to be registered at, but the system was that the pool allocated seamen to crews as required. It was also required that seamen could be sent to another port to make up crews.

The new regulations, which came into effect in May 1941, were

prompted by increasing shortages of manpower. Despite the whole-
sale retraining of stewards made surplus to requirements by the
slump in passenger traffic, ships were being held up for want of deck
crewmen and engineers. Although it guaranteed pay between
voyages, the pool system was resented because of its element of
compulsion – seamen were no longer able to choose between good
and bad ships. In addition, the terms of a new Essential Work Order
now prevented anyone from leaving the Merchant Navy for jobs
ashore, as a number had done.

At the end of leave you had to report to the pool every day,
until you got a ship. After a few days if you hadn't got a job
you were put on 'standby', which meant that you had to report
twice each day and be ready packed for a 'pier head jump' –
this was the term used for joining a ship in the river on her way
out.

They sent me to join a tanker at Ellesmere Port, the *El Mirlo*.
There was a series of bad air raids at the time on Merseyside,
and in one of the night raids just before I sailed the house my
family lived in at Wallasey was badly damaged by blast. When I
got home the windows and part of the walls were blown in, and
in order to sleep I had to shake glass from the bed. A lot of
people had been killed and I remember on the following day
when I passed, workers were removing bodies from one of the
smashed houses.

The day I was due to sail my father was searching for another
place to live, and said he would write to me with the address.
We pulled out into the Mersey, which by this time was getting
quite a collection of wrecks from mines and bombing, and
sailed for the Clyde where we anchored in Loch Long to form
convoy. I think there were about thirty-five ships in the convoy,
with a very sparse escort. About two days out we were joined
by an armed merchant cruiser. These were small passenger
liners converted for escort duties and manned by a mix of RN
and merchant seamen. The merchant seamen had to volunteer
and sign special articles, designated T124X. They were virtually
in the RN.

After what seemed only hours after she joined the convoy we
were attacked, and two ships torpedoed. The corvettes raced

about dropping depth charges, but as soon as they were in the area where the two ships had been hit, another ship in a different part of the convoy was torpedoed.

The following morning it was calm weather and quite warm; at about ten o'clock I was out on the deck having a cigarette, watching the other ships zig-zag, when there was a tremendous flash followed by a bang and the ship on our port side heeled over and then righted herself. Within a minute the whole midships section was in flames, and as she drifted astern I watched two seamen jump off the stern – at least one jumped, the other did a magnificent swallow dive. Another ship was hit on our starboard side, and she fell back out of the convoy sinking fast. The depth charges were exploding quite close to us and the bangs were terrific. We were always told that one of the ships at the rear of the convoy was deputed to be a rescue ship to pick up survivors. I was never in that position, so I don't know if it was true or just a palliative for our nerves. There was no further action that day, and we thought we'd lost the U-boats. The convoy carried on until in the late evening there were two more explosions and two more ships had been hit. At this point the convoy broke up and scattered.

We called at Nassau in the Bahamas and then sailed through the Caribbean to Aruba in the Dutch West Indies where we loaded. This was a nice island, and goods were very cheap. I remember I bought six Arrow shirts, made in the USA, for about four shillings each and two sets of silk pyjamas for five shillings each.

After loading we headed north, called at Cuba for water and then sailed for Halifax, Nova Scotia. This was not a popular place for seamen. I don't think the town was much, and beer was rationed to, I think, two glasses per day. My main memories of it are that it always seemed cold, and the mournful hooters on the trains. We left in convoy for the UK, to the Mersey. I don't think we had any interference on that trip. I only remember the convoy steering round some icebergs up by the Belle Isle Straits. We arrived in the Mersey safely and were told to proceed to the Shell refinery at Ellesmere Port to discharge cargo. There was a letter for me telling me that my home was now in Liverpool and, while the ship was discharging, I got a ferry home. When I got back the following morning it was to find that the ship had been damaged in an air raid. A bomb had landed on the jetty within yards of the ship, and the splinters had torn holes in her bows. Fortunately though, most of the crew had been ashore so no one was hurt.

With the *El Mirlo* out of service for repairs, he found himself re-allocated to other vessels, including a requisitioned ocean liner, the *Pasteur*.

The *Pasteur* was a French liner built for cruising from Marseilles to the West Indies, but she had never entered service and the British took her over when France capitulated to the Germans. She was a beautiful ship, but her lines were spoilt by the single funnel which, I think, was the biggest funnel ever used on any ship. It always seemed out of proportion. She was sailing under the flag of Cunard White Star and was ferrying American soldiers to the UK. I worked on her for six months, running between New York and Liverpool. We always sailed alone and never saw any sign of U-boat activity, except on one occasion we passed through a lot of wreckage from what I presume had been an enemy attack on a convoy. This was off Northern Ireland as we were homeward bound. I believe the turn round at each end of a voyage was about forty-eight hours. Part of the time the crew was given leave.

New York was never bothered by rationing of anything, and it was possible to buy goods to take home. Unfortunately crew members were restricted to an allowance of only ten dollars a week, and in order.to get extra it became a habit for members of ships' crews to go to Bellevue Hospital and sell their blood. A pint of blood was worth five dollars.

I think almost every cinema and theatre in New York reserved a number of seats for service personnel, and these tickets were issued free. Merchant seamen were included in this category, and certainly I saw some wonderful shows at that time, shows that were in some cases booked for months ahead.

My immediate boss on the *Pasteur* wasn't a very nice man, and I had constant trouble with him. We had heated arguments, and four times I was logged [fined] ten shillings.

At the end of six months I was sacked when we reached Liverpool with the threat of a DR in my discharge book. At about ten in the morning, a couple of hours after tying up, I had to report to the Shipping Master to sign off. It caused problems when I refused to sign without a hearing. There were arguments between the Shipping Master, my boss and the Staff Captain, and it was not until two o'clock that I was persuaded by the Shipping Master to sign off with the proviso that I signed under protest and with a guarantee that there would be no DR.

The only good thing was that my boss, who lived in Southampton, would not have got home that trip! I just had to be sure never to sail with him again!

4

DOCKYARD HANDS

For the Royal Navy, rearmament began in earnest with the 1936–37 Estimates. These sanctioned the ordering of no less than four new big ships (the aircraft carriers *Illustrious* and *Victorious* together with the 14 inch gun battleships *King George V* and *Prince of Wales*), two 6 inch gun cruisers, five air defence cruisers and double the usual number of submarines and destroyers.

Although they meant, of course, that the government considered war more likely, these orders were understandably welcome news for depressed regions like Tyneside and the River Clyde.

The famous names in British shipbuilding – Vickers-Armstrong at Barrow and Walker, Hawthorn Leslie at Hebburn, Swan Hunter at Wallsend, John Brown at Clydebank, Yarrow at Scotstoun, Fairfield at Govan, Denny Bros. at Dumbarton – tended to dominate their surrounding areas, so that the fortunes of a whole community were often inextricably linked with those of the local yard.

After the outbreak of war, the crash building programme for cheap, mass-produced vessels such as antisubmarine escorts also filled up the order books of the many smaller firms dotted around the country.

Roy Barclay joined one such firm, Charles Hill & Sons of Bristol, as an apprentice in 1938, and was able to watch its labour force expanding rapidly to meet the new demand.

When the war started the yard took on about forty women workers, who seemed to spend more time putting paint on their faces than anything else. They did do a good job, though, once they'd settled down.

The number of men employed in peacetime was 300, rising to 600 men and women during the war.

I was on what was called 'new work' – corvettes, Flower class. The yard built eight of them, all launched with no trouble as regards air raids. I think the first to be finished was HMS *Clematis*, K.36 – yard no. 278. I remember the crow's nest was a wooden beer barrel, and the chippie who worked on the job got drunk on the beer fumes inside! After the corvettes we started building frigates – a bit bigger, with more speed, more crew, and so on. All these ships were rivet-built, and to work inside them was very bad as regards the noise. In the winter when the ships were on the slipways it was so cold you had a job to use your tools. Most men wore gloves or mittens, but the cold wind used to come through the rivet holes in the steel plates and down through the open deck. If it was pouring with rain you just got wet.

The men used to start work at 7.30, stop at 9.00 for quarter of an hour teabreak, 9.15 to 12 noon, 12 noon to 1.00 p.m. for dinner, 1.00 to 5.30. You could carry on till 8.00 p.m. if you wanted to. Not many did. You were paid on a Friday – when you passed out through the time office you shouted out your number and you were handed a round tin with your notes rolled up and change at the bottom. You checked your wages outside the time office and threw the tin into a big wicker basket.

Sometimes we fitters were sent by lorry to Avonmouth to work on ships discharging cargo there – repairs to engines, repairs to boilers, or deck steam winches. What would happen was as soon as we arrived on board the chargehand fitter would have a word with the ship's Chief Engineer, who would give him a list of all the repairs to be done. A lot of them were dirty jobs, but I still enjoyed working on the ships.

Later Roy joined the Merchant Navy, so had a chance to see shipyards from the crews' point of view. Relations between the two groups were rarely cordial, as submariner *Albert Lines* recalls:

There wasn't much love lost between the Navy and the dock-yard mateys. I don't know why. And yet on the other hand I've stood by two submarines that were being built, both in the Vickers yard at Barrow-in-Furness, and the workmen there, we used to get on with them quite well. They used to come to sea with us. When I was at Barrow, we never went to sea and dived – they had a dock up there called Grantham Dock, and we used to go into that. It was so deep that we could dive, and if there was any fault we could find it before we put to sea. They didn't do that at Cammell's [Cammell Laird, Birkenhead]. There it was straight into Liverpool Bay.

Any vessel under construction or refit was a dangerous place for the unwary, as *Eric Tubb* found when he reported aboard his first ship at Devonport Dockyard.

I went to the destroyer *Wolverine*, which was in major refit. The ship was ghostlike, and you took your life in your hands balancing along an iron girder. They just took the whole guts out of the ship – it was just a shell there, the whole boilers were lifted out, and to get forward to our little messdeck you walked along a girder like that, with a sheer drop. In a naval dockyard there's a thousand and one pipes and wires going everywhere. Many, many sailors lost their lives in the dockyard dry docks.

Yet strangely, I loved it. I love trades, and there was all the workshops, carpenters' workshops, shipwrights, and there was the smell of everything. Devonport dockyard even had its own train service. Trains used to go from South yard to North yard.

Devonport was one of the six great Royal Dockyards, the others being Portsmouth, Chatham, Sheerness, Pembroke and Rosyth. All of them, like the private yards, had experienced a lean time in the depression years of the 1920s and early 30s, when Pembroke and Rosyth had in fact been mothballed to cut down some of the over-capacity. Now, of course, the order books were full again and all six Royal yards were taking on additional staff.

Chatham, which *Frank Wright* joined in August 1942, could trace its history back to Tudor times. Nelson's *Victory* had been built there. Little did he realize that it would remain his workplace for the next forty-one years.

I entered the dockyard as a general hand, before passing an examination for an apprenticeship at the age of seventeen and a half. Numerous trades were on offer, but I chose plumbing – for the reason that when the war ended and redundancies were made, I'd be in a better position to obtain work in the outside world! As it turns out, I'm pleased to say this never happened.

My 'skipper' was an expert on copper items, and we used to do a lot of 2 inch voice pipe work. The first ship I ever worked on was a cruiser, for which we did all the voice pipes in the gun turrets and the cordite and shell handling rooms. Most of the pipes we bent into shape by filling them with sand and then heating them on open coke fires. During the blackout the ventilation was poor, with smoke and coke fumes filling the workshop, which had a rather low pitched roof.

I then changed instructors and went onto submarines, both new construction and refits; 'S' class and 'T' class. It was grotty working on submarines – with refits you were dismantling the insides in a confined space, with pipes, wires, floor plates taken up, so many people crammed into a small area. It was most uncomfortable. And with new construction it was very noisy. Draughts and winds in the winter, even on a covered slipway. I'm happy to say the noise never had any long-term effects on me, but I know many employees suffered hearing trouble in later life.

Another industrial hazard was the effect of working with asbestos. This was used a great deal in various forms for insulation of boiler pipes and things. Working conditions were always hard during the war, and stores were in short supply – to obtain such a thing as a new file was like asking for the Earth!

And if you were late clocking on, say twice in a fortnight, even if it was only a matter of minutes, you were liable to be sent home for the half day without pay. Unless of course you could prove it was due to enemy action or breakdown in public transport. Chargehands were always on duty keeping an eye on things in the workshop, with sometimes an inspector walking around. Someone looking over your shoulder all the time.

We employed about 10,500 to 10,700 men during the war. We had four canteens located in various parts of the yard, so the workmen didn't have to travel too far for a meal, though they were very 'utility' in the service provided.

As a lucrative target, the sprawling dockyard at Chatham suffered numerous tip-and-run raids by the Luftwaffe, especially during the Battle of Britain.

One night raid hit the factory where we built submarine engines, and killed quite a number of workmen. We also had the raid when they went after the cruiser *Ajax*, under refit. They missed the ship, but the blast tipped a steam crane over and peppered the driver – Weaver, I think his name was – with shrapnel. He lived near me. He never fully recovered from that.

Much to his surprise Frank was kept on after the war, becoming a union representative in 1963. He accepted early retirement in August 1983 at the age of fifty-eight and a half, when his yard had only a few more months of existence left.

The closure came as a shock to many, although I half expected it. The Foundry had shut down in the 1960s when the foundry work was transferred to Portsmouth, and the Main Stores Distribution moved away in the 1970s, so they'd been taking bits away long before the closure was announced by the then Defence Minister, John Nott.

Chatham finally closed in 1984.

Well, there's not a great deal left in the dockyard now apart from the historic section. The lower basins now accommodate container ships, but the main part of the yard has simply been bulldozed to the ground.

It's funny you know, I never originally intended to work in a dockyard – it was just that events resulted in me doing so.

I made a lot of friends in my time there, and I still see a lot of them in the Chatham Dockyard Historical Society. At least that's worth something.

5

WAVY NAVY

On mobilization the Royal Navy was swelled to almost double its peacetime strength by calling back former servicemen – principally the officers on the Retired and Emergency Lists (regular officers who had previously retired or resigned) and the ratings of the Royal Fleet Reserve (ratings who had finished their time with the regulars), plus RN pensioners under the age of fifty-five – and by adding the officers and men of the Royal Naval Reserve and the Royal Naval Volunteer Reserve.

The RNR consisted of professional seafarers, many of whom simply exchanged their merchant ships for warships on the outbreak of hostilities. The RNVR were weekend and evening sailors, who often joined because of enthusiasm for the Navy, and who learned the rudiments of seamanship in their free time. Both were distinguished from the 'real' Navy by wavy rank rings on their uniforms, hence their universal nickname of 'Wavy Navy'.

Usually friendly rivalries emerged from the presence in British ships of these disparate groups of sailors, exemplified perhaps in the oft-heard joke that the RNR were sailors trying to be gentlemen, and the RNVR were gentlemen trying to be sailors.

Reservists were quickly placed aboard warships to augment their complement of regulars, but there was also an arm of the Royal Navy which was exclusively their own. The Royal Naval Patrol Service, previously known as the Trawler Section of the RNR, provided ships and crews throughout the war for dangerous and unglamorous tasks like minesweeping and convoy escort. From the outset the background of its crews – 'What the Navy did was requisition all these fishing trawlers, shove a round hat on these chaps' heads, and say you're in the Navy now!' as one participant put it – gave the RNPS an approach quite unlike the rigidly-disciplined spit-and-polish of the RN proper.

Charlie Wines volunteered for the Patrol Service soon after the war began.

I don't come from a seafaring family, though my father was in the fish-curing trade. At the age of fourteen I went to work as an office boy for a well known firm of yacht builders by the name of Woodnutt & Co. After ten years of learning about boats I left Woodnutt's because I could advance no more until someone died, and I was married with a young daughter. So I asked for, and got, a job on board a yacht of 350 tons called the *Anna Marie*, and did a two-month cruise of the Baltic – Denmark, Sweden, Norway, the Isle of Rugen, and Germany, through the Kiel Canal. That was in 1938. Our owner then bought a larger yacht, the *Vita II*, which had belonged to Tommy Sopwith, who had taken the America's Cup challenger *Endeavour* to America and back.[4] After a further three-month cruise in the Mediterranean the wife didn't want me to go to sea again, so I got a job ashore.

When war broke out I used to run a boat to Southsea and pick up servicemen coming home to the Isle of Wight for their weekend leave. Then in January-February 1940 or thereabouts I went to Portsmouth without the wife's knowledge and volunteered for the Royal Naval Patrol Service. My papers came through the end of July – railway warrant to Lowestoft [headquarters of the RNPS] – and within ten days I was commissioning HM Trawler *St Zeno* in the King George Dock in Hull as Seaman Steward Wines LT/JX 203859.

We had a motley crew of about thirty-six, and only about fifteen of us had been to sea before. *St Zeno* was a new trawler of 600 tons, coal burning, with triple expansion engines. After a short time working up at Tobermory we went off to Londonderry and Belfast running convoys, mostly northern ones to Iceland and so on. Then we had a change of skippers, from a

---

[4] Sir Thomas Sopwith, aviation pioneer and founder of the Sopwith Company. The *Endeavour* was one of the famous J class racing yachts.

Lieutenant-Commander, RNR to a Lieutenant, RNVR – who came from Glasgow. He was a damn fine seaman and a good skipper; I liked him.

We had more than our share of sinkings and picking up survivors, especially tankers. One convoy we lost three tankers and some other freighters – it was terrible to see chaps in the sea trying to dive under the flames, only to come up in the middle. We managed to pick up eleven, but before we got back to Belfast two of those died. The burnt ones we covered with flour, which seemed to ease their pain.

When America entered the war in December 1941, the German U-boats moved in on her unprotected coastal shipping, and British escorts (and their experienced crews) were quick to follow.

In February 1942 I was recalled from leave. When I got on board the Old Man told me to top up all stores, hard tack and all, but I got nothing out of him about destination. We set off with two other trawlers, tangled with half a merchantman in mid-Atlantic – she flattened our port quarter – and we ended up in St John's, Newfoundland. Stayed two nights and then off again, this time through the ice fields to Halifax. Pretty frightening to hear the ice floes scraping along the ship's side! And then on to Cape Cod where we damaged our Asdic dome – two of us with lines tied around us went over the side and managed to get it freed, but we had to call in to Boston for repairs. As we were coming alongside a docker called out to ask where we were from, and was surprised to hear from Paddy on our forecastle that we came from England. How had we got across? Paddy's reply was 'By ploodie taxi ye ploodie fool, how else did ye tink we came!' From Boston we went on to Brooklyn, New York and finished up operating out of Norfolk, Virginia. Our run was from Norfolk to Key West, calling at times at Charleston, Miami and places down the coast.

Did you get on with the Americans?

Well, I must say that when we got away out into the interior everything was fine, and everyone claimed to have come from the old country or had relations there. But as for the sailors, not so good. We found them brash and argumentative, and they bragged all the time about the subs they'd sunk, though in reality when there was a blow coming on or hard weather in general the signal would come through for US ships to return to harbour and British ships to carry on. There were twenty-one trawlers went over to the States in 42, and three were sunk in collision with US ships – need I say more? [He shows me the details – *St Cathan*, lost 11 April 1942; *Senatuer Duhamel*, lost 6 May 1942; and *Pentland Firth*, lost 19 September 1942] The Yankee navy you can keep.

We lost the *Bedfordshire* the night of 11/12 May. We had the sweep outside till midnight and the *Bedfordshire* took the inside sweep; at midnight we changed stations and that was the last we saw or heard of her – not a peep. But later we found out that she was sunk by *U.558* off Cape Lookout.

We left in November and went down to Trinidad to pick up three tankers loaded with high octane fuel, us, *Stella Polaris* and *Coventry City*. We were lucky, we took them to Freetown and never had a sniff of the opposition. At Freetown we picked up a floating crane and took that down to Walfish Bay, then on to arrive in Cape Town on Christmas Eve 1942. After that we were on convoys up to Port Elizabeth, East London, Durban, Mombasa and Trincomalee. We had some rough times off Cape Agulhas – German, Italian *and* Japanese subs to contend with!

When war broke out, the strength of the RNVR had stood at roughly 1,000 officers and 7,000 ratings. Although the number of officers expanded enormously during the war, in fact there was no more recruitment into the permanent RNVR for the duration – all wartime officers' appointments were temporary. Most of them, like *Les Roberts*, entered the Royal Navy as ratings and were then recommended for Reserve commissions.

I joined the Royal Navy shortly after the outbreak of war because I was mad about everything to do with the sea, particularly the Royal Navy. My family on my father's side had been seafaring since way back – owning and sailing their own sailing ships in the last century. My grandfather, my father and his twin brother were all marine engineers. Until I was eleven we lived in Holyhead, my father being on the cross-channel ships to Ireland. I would spend a goodly part of my school holidays on the ship, crossing and recrossing the Irish Sea and loving every minute of it.

I left grammar school after a year in the lower VI. I had no thoughts of going to university and, indeed, I was not natural university material. In those days you did arts or sciences, but I was a hybrid; I revelled in maths and languages but spent my days at the very bottom of the form in all sciences. Today, of course, you can read something like a BA in maths, french and ludo! I did think of going to sea, but my father painted such a horrendous picture of life as an apprentice that I was dissuaded. I became a junior local government officer with the Liverpool Education Service.

However, when war broke out I said to my father that it was going to be the Navy for me, come what may. He smiled: 'Anything else would have to be over my dead body.' It was some years before I realized the real reason for his earlier attitude. Like many mariners, the depression of the 1930s had hit him hard. For years we had been living (and I had been educated) on his capital; he just could not have afforded the premium for a cadetship with a reputable shipping company. This was in keeping with all my upbringing – the fact that it had been a struggle for my parents was always kept from me.

It was months before the Navy needed seamen. There were vacancies for stokers, cooks and stewards, but these were of no interest to me. Finally the Chief Petty Officer at the recruiting office, after a lengthy interview, said that seamen were now required and made a note on my application form that I was possible officer material.

I trained at HMS *Raleigh* – a shore base at Torpoint – for three months, learning the basics of seamanship and of course the mysterious language of the Navy, where cocoa was 'kai' and even the floor of the barracks was a deck. During this time notices went up on a board now and again, asking for volunteers for this specialization or that. With a few others I was drawn to this close range anti-aircraft gunnery course, and put my name down. I was accepted and at the end of the *Raleigh* course went on to the gunnery school at Whale Island for another three months. In those days your main hope was to

survive the discipline there! Everything was done at the double
– you never walked, not even from one classroom to another.
Parade ground drills would have been perfectly adequate preparation for the Foreign Legion!

Anyway, I did survive and eventually I was drafted to coastal
forces at Yarmouth. After about a year of this, the CO sent for
me and said that my service certificate had only just come to
hand, and that it was marked that I might be considered for
officer training. Where it had been I don't know! I had given up
any idea of being considered for a commission. Anyway, he
arranged for me to go up before a regional preliminary selection board, and they were satisfied to pass me on to the full
Admiralty board. I walked into that room and was simply
dazzled by the amount of gold braid there. It was awesome!
However, the Vice Admiral President was very charming –
'Anxious?' I said that I was *very* anxious. 'Then join the club',
he said kindly, 'We are most anxious that you prove yourself
suitable to go on for training. We need chaps very badly.' The
President was a remarkable man. He asked me a question
concerning charts. I didn't know the answer but tried to work it
out. I gave the correct answer, but having spotted my hesitation
he asked 'Scout's honour now, did you work that one out or
was it a guess?' I told him I had tried to see the logic of the
answer. 'Good', he smiled. Then, when I answered a question
wrongly, he explained why I was wrong and asked me another
question embodying the same principle. I got it right this time.

Miracles happening far more often than people imagine, I got
through.

The Admiralty had taken over the picturesque Lancing
College near Worthing as a training establishment, renaming it
HMS *King Alfred*. The course was of three months' duration,
hence the name given to the RNVR Sub-Lieutenants it churned
out – 'Ninety day wonders'. Actually there was a further three
weeks' training, now as an officer, if you got through the
course. Plus, if you add 90×4 hours' private study every evening, the course actually extends by quite a bit!

Navigation, seamanship, gunnery, signals, explosives, fleet
manoeuvres and squarebashing made for a very intensive
course indeed, and we quickly realized that the best way to

study privately was to establish little study groups. It is no way to practise morse signalling or semaphore by looking at illustrations in a book. We would sit in groups, each of us tossing in questions on anything – the wires used for minesweeping, colour codes on ammunition, orders for lowering a boat, you name it.

There was a huge mock-up of a ship's forecastle there. A group would gather round it, each person taking turns at playing the role of the various people involved in anchoring – CO, Forecastle Officer, Blacksmith [in big ships] and so on. Galley slaves had nothing on us.

One of my outstanding recollections of this time is of a sticky August afternoon; a Chief Petty Officer is explaining how to strip a Lewis gun. Having spent a year cleaning four of them every twenty-four hours, naturally, my attention wanders to the two aircraft that can be seen through the window. And then the crafty Chief's voice: 'The gun will now be assembled by Cadet Rating Roberts.' I stand behind the various parts laid out on the table, and my sense of mischief breaks surface. I take off the black neck scarf that Jolly Jack wears, and put it round my eyes – 'While I'm about it, I might as well tell you how these parts can be identified by feel. You may sometime have to strip and reassemble such a weapon in the dark if there's been some serious fault with it!' I went on to do it, pointing out the shape of locking devices by feel, that one part went into another with a twist of the wrist to the right twice and so on, until the gun was back in one piece. Just then the bugle sounded off for the afternoon cuppa. The CPO said 'The class will assemble at 15.15 hours, when Cadet Rating Roberts will demonstrate the very difficult process of removing a bullet that has jammed in the breech. You will pay the strictest attention and do exactly as he tells you to, otherwise the round could be fired and one of you may not see the end of the course!' which I suppose was one way of accepting my expertise without actually having to say so!

Finally there was a three-day exam to face, preceded by a 'mock' one. The bane of my school days, pre-exam nerves, struck again. The fear of failing was just awful. In the mocks I made the most dreadful hash of things that was possible. Six out of 100 for navigation – my favourite! A shameful return to the lower deck was facing me. Shaking like a leaf, going to bed the night before the exam proper, some inner voice said that if all the worrying I was doing ended up with 6 out of 100 for things, why not go to sleep and just have a bash at it the following morning; I couldn't do worse than I had so far. And with that I put my head on the pillow and went to sleep.

I actually went into the first exam whistling under my breath. It was navigation. The charts were already spread out on trestle tables with chart pens and inks ready to tackle the problem. I read the problem through – piece of cake. I wasn't all that bothered even when an invigilator kicked the trestle legs away, sending the coloured inks everywhere.

I compared notes with everyone after the paper. I had ended up in the right place seemingly. Other papers came and went; then came ship handling. Question 7 – funny how you remember such details – was to tow another ship into harbour and berth her alongside the quay. There was little room to spare because of others berthed ahead and astern of the space allotted to your charge. Like everyone else I was foxed – to manoeuvre a ship swinging on the end of a tow? I had completed the paper but for this. Looking around the room, I could see others surreptitiously mouthing 'Question 7?' to their chums. Time was ticking by, and then it hit me. We had done it in the coastal forces! 'Towing' is an all-embracing term – it includes making the other ship fast *alongside your own*. My little pen was almost throwing off sparks as I scrambled the answer down – the engine movements, the helm movements, the lashings making both ships fast to each other. Phew! I just made it.

Outside the room afterwards everyone was asking everyone else whether they had done Question 7. The class swot had, of course, but I was the only other. Everyone crowded round the invigilator, who was leaving the room with the papers. How was Question 7 meant to be done? The heartening answer was 'You start by towing the other ship alongside your own . . .' My spirits soared – I might even get through this lot, and I did. About half way up – or down – the pass list did me. The bottom would have done, in fact! I was commissioned as a Temporary Acting Sub-Lieutenant, RNVR. As a friend of mine remarked at the time, 'Anything lower than that has to be on *their* side!' Actually I dropped the 'Acting' on reaching twenty-one, which made it a shade more respectable.

I must add that there were two other aspects which were under constant appraisal throughout our training. One was power of command, assessed by the way we took parades, boat drills, captained gun crews and so on. The other was whether or not we displayed OLQ – officer-like qualities. Did we use a fork like a spoon to eat peas, or did we harpoon them with the prongs of the fork? Oh yes, we were under observation all the time. I got one hell of a telling off for dropping a cigarette butt on a path. I was told, and I have never forgotten it, to 'pick up my filth!'

The position of RNVR officers aboard ship was not always easy. At the beginning of the war everyone regarded them as little more than enthusiastic amateurs. By the time I gained my commission, RNVR officers were far more plentiful and, indeed, by the end of the war were in the majority.

In fact, by 1945 RNVR officers outnumbered their regular colleagues by a ratio of four to one.

For my part, I found the vast majority of Chiefs and Petty Officers appreciated that we ourselves would have wished for more training. They realized that we needed all the support we could get – and gave it. Though there was always the odd snide smartarse who behaved differently. The most dubious people were often the 'Hostilities Only' ratings. This was understandable. Being so very green themselves, they hoped their lives were in the hands of officers who knew what they were doing.

However, we learned. Sometimes by our mistakes, but we learned. Perhaps the proudest day of my entire life dawned two and a half years after being commissioned. Our chief Bosun's Mate was proceeding on shore leave, resplendent in a brand new uniform. God, he looked smart. I said to him as he went over the gangway: 'Portsmouth here I come! Take a look at what a *real* sailor looks like!' He smiled with pleasure as he saluted, adding 'And it takes one to know one!'

I wouldn't swap that moment for a knighthood.

But many regular ratings too were deeply scathing about Wavy Navy officers and their competence to command. Engine Room Artificer *Les Mason* was one such sceptic.

Under wartime conditions a very rapid expansion of the Navy was necessary, and of course the replacement of personnel lost in action meant that normal training wasn't possible. There was also an ingress of weekend yachting enthusiasts, and we all know that many of these types are more familiar with the clubroom than the sea. These were the 'Wavy Navy' types that I had the misfortune to come across. It was one such clown that wrecked my LST [tank landing ship]. He'd tried hard to do so many times before – the crew thought he was doing hydrographic work since in spite of good charts he always seemed to find sand or gravel banks, causing problems in the engine room when the circulating pumps sucked in sand and discharged it into the main engine condensers, not a recommended procedure for good maintenance. Bombay harbour must have been well documented, as we had at least six strandings in the few days that we were there.

His best effort was the landings on the Malay coast, where our function was to land Army tanks and support services. It was spectacular. Having previously ordered all ballast tanks to be emptied we hit the beach with engines running at full speed and succeeded in placing the ship's bows right between the only two palm trees near the water. This brilliant navigation meant that we couldn't open the bow doors, and consequently the guns on the Army's tanks, which should have been our main armament in the event of the Japanese challenging the landings, couldn't be used . . .

There was also a reluctance to accept reservists as equals on the lower deck. *Fred Holliday* was a rating in the pre-war RNVR who experienced the regulars' disdain, bordering on outright hostility.

I joined when I was working in London as a clerk in the City. There were two or three of us, all quite young then, and one joined the RNVR which was at HMS *President*, lying alongside the Embankment at Blackfriars, so he encouraged the rest of us to join as well. We had nothing else to do when we left our offices at five o'clock, so we did.

It was interesting and we learned a little bit about signalling and guns and things like that. To us office clerks it was completely different, apart from which there was a very good little canteen on board. And they were great. We used to take trips from Blackfriars Bridge down the river to Greenhithe, rowing all the way in whalers, and spend the weekend at Greenhithe.

And when war was anticipated you were mobilized?

We were. I've got a photograph of myself on the very night I was called up, in my uniform, outside my house. My dad and my mum were so terribly excited. It was before the war had been declared. A friend of my father's who had a motor car – there weren't many about in those good old days – took me up to Blackfriars. There we were mobilized and I was sent with a little party of twelve other London RNVRs to Victoria Station, with our kitbags – immense kitbags – and hammocks, a kitbag on one shoulder and a hammock on the other. We were put on a train, and when we arrived at Portland in the early hours of the morning we were completely overwhelmed. We were taken down to the docks and ushered into a boat that took us out to this battleship.

You were assumed to be trained and ready?

Well, we were partly trained I suppose you could say. Partially trained, but only in terms of having learned a certain amount of climbing the rigging – there was one thing about HMS *President* along Blackfriars Embankment, she was a big tall ship with rigging, a lot of rigging, and we were taught how to climb it. Never ever experienced it after that! But this experience of going down in the middle of the night to somewhere you'd never been before, and being taken out by a small boat to a battleship lying in the harbour. We'd never seen anything like it, except for our training during the years before when we'd perhaps gone on board *Nelson* or *Rodney* on fleet exercises, when London RNVRs were treated as special! But this time it wasn't special, it was for real. I was taken down these ladders, struggling. Hammock, kitbag. Oh, didn't know where I was. Somebody said to me 'That's it mate. This is your mess'. Lying on the mess table was a seaman. I've still got all this bloody stuff on my shoulders, and he opens his eyes and says 'Whadda you want, mate?' I said, 'I've come with me stuff; I've been allocated to this mess.' And he says 'When you're in a seaman's mess, mate, yer takes yer fucking 'at orff!'

He was, as I learned later on, the leading hand of the mess, so he was entitled to treat the others as he liked [laughs]. So that was my introduction. Of course they were regulars, weren't they? And they hated us – they thought we were trying to take their jobs.

How did the hostility express itself?

In their attitude towards us. It was remarkable, looking back after all these years.

A week or so later when we were sitting on the messdeck, the news came through over the broadcasting system that war had been declared. The regulars: 'Wha! We'll soon see them off! Be over in a fortnight!'

I was always in trouble. I was a bit of a rebel, in fact I still am in a way. So eventually I asked my divisional officer if I could apply for special duties, and he said 'All right, I'll put your name down.' So strangely enough a few days later there was a call came over the tannoy – would Ordinary Seaman Holliday go to his divisional officer's office. Which I did, and he said 'I've got a gentleman here who would like to speak to you – go and have a word with him and tell me what you think.'

The stranger said 'Do you feel as if you'd like to do something different?' I said yes, I did. He said 'You look as if you've done a bit of boxing.' He looked at me nose. I said I hadn't done any boxing really, but I didn't mind a fight. Then he said 'Would you care to join a ship that's rather unusual? Would you be prepared to accept the fact that if you're captured you could be shot?' Well, that shook me, didn't it, shook me rigid. But it didn't take me long to reply 'Yes, certainly Sir', and that evening I had several people come along to me and say 'Get your bags packed mate!' Do this and do that. It was all so secret. 'You've got a pair of overalls to put on? Well get them on.' No uniform, no cap, nothing. And secretly I was ushered over the side of the battleship onto the quay at Gibraltar there, walked along the quay about fifty yards and there's this little old merchant packet. The fellow says 'Right, up the gangway mate.' There she was, an old 1500 ton merchantman, and all I could see was gundecks, torpedo tubes, and messdecks for a crew of 130! She was a Q-ship, the *City of Durban*. She'd been gutted and 4 inch guns, torpedo tubes, this that and the other fitted – she was a floating gunship.

Our purpose was to deceive the enemy, to invite U-boats to come up and challenge us. The operation then would be that we would just pretend to be an ordinary merchant packet, invite the sub to lay off, and then the order would be given to 'abandon ship' – we had an abandon ship party of which I was one – the lifeboats would be lowered and the abandon ship party would pull away. Then the U-boat would approach, or she would allow crewmen to appear above decks, and the order would be given to drop flaps – out with the guns and that was that. Amazing operation really.

When we left Gib, we were sent down to the Cape, Simonstown, and on the way down the coast of Africa we had to refuel at Freetown, Sierra Leone. There was a cruiser, a destroyer and several other ships there at the time, and they were having a naval boxing championship. Well, a cruiser carried about 600 men and we had a crew of 130, but our skipper was a fitness fanatic. He used to have us up on deck every day, and he was also a keen boxer – he'd been training four boxers at the various weights coming down the coast. He entered our four lads in this championship, and we won with two of them. We were only a little old merchant ship, remember, and the sailors in Freetown were saying 'What's this bloody thing the *City of Durban*?' [laughs].

Was he a good Captain? Did you like him?

Yes, we did indeed. As a matter of fact we didn't only like him, we thought he was the greatest. He was a great character. Commander H.G. Hopper, RN.

So did a U-boat ever take the bait?

We were never attacked, though we were followed many a time. We had our Asdic operator, Ping we called him, and Ping would be saying 'Yep, we're being followed – we've got a U-boat up our arse!' It would go on for days, but what can you do? You've got to wait – the first move has to come from the sub, not from us. Otherwise it loses all its element of surprise. So this went on for days. The Skipper used to give us a daily report, on how we were being shadowed, but there was nothing we could do about it. We just had to wait and see what was going to happen. In the event nothing ever did. Strange, isn't it?

Was it frustrating?

I don't know about frustrating. As a crew I suppose we all wanted something to happen, but nothing did. Nothing we could do about it. [He shows me a copy of his Q-ship's magazine, typed on very flimsy paper, containing stories, poems and cartoons usually featuring Popeye and Olive]. That was the very last official monthly programme written by one of our CPOs on board, when we were told by the Admiralty that's it, you've had your time. It was called *The White Elephant* because we weren't sinking any submarines, we were sailing the high seas as white elephants. So we were told to pay off and become Royal Navy again, and fly the White Ensign.

Even after reservists (or at least the need for their presence in wartime) became more widely accepted, the issue of their promotion remained a touchy subject among the regulars, as chef *Lou Garcon* discovered.

I've been in catering all my life. They used to call me a bloody foreigner, being a Channel Islander. I used to say to the English chaps I worked with, well, you might call me a foreigner, I said, but actually you belong to us because my ancestor the Duke of Normandy came over here and tanned the hides off you bastards!

I served my apprenticeship in the Grand Hotel in Paris as a chef, and then worked over here at the Park Lane and the Grosvenor House. I joined the Channel Islands Society in London, and at one of their dinners I was introduced to Joe Symons, who was the catering superintendent of the Union Castle Company. He asked whether I had considered going to sea. I said yes, I quite fancied it, and within a matter of weeks he wrote to me to say that if I wanted it there was a vacancy for me with the Union Castle Line, working in the first class galleys for the passengers.

And you joined the RNVR?

That's right. The only rank in the RNVR at the time was Cook, or Steward, but I wanted to go into something that I knew about. I soon went from Cook to Leading Cook to Petty Officer Cook; as a matter of fact within a few months I was recommended for Warrant Cook, which was the highest rank that a cook could become. But I was RNVR, and that got the backs of two or three of the Warrant Cooks in the Navy up – it had taken them fifteen years to get to that rank, so they didn't want somebody like me to get it. Eventually they brought in the Warrant Catering Officer rank, and I was one of the first. In fact I was the only RNVR Catering Officer appointed to a carrier during the war.

However, his wartime service began aboard something rather smaller.

HMS *Wolborough* was one of the fastest trawlers that we had, and the Admiralty had commandeered her. Twenty-eight of a crew, plus a dog [shows me photos], I'm not in these, of course, because I took 'em. We were credited with sinking at least one submarine. Now this is a depth charge attack [photo] on an Italian sub, and that's Commander Ramsay in his khaki shorts and shirtsleeves. He's looking to see if debris comes up.

I joined the *Wolborough* in Dover. When Tobruk got surrounded we were converted to the Tobruk run. That's us [photo] in Tobruk under the nets. We were on that run for six months, from the time that Tobruk was surrounded.

My action station on board [photo]. I had the port side Lewis guns alongside the bridge. The Tobruk run was escorting tank landing craft loaded with tanks up to Tobruk for when they were going to do their breakout. Eventually when the British counterattack came along the road from Mersa Matruh and got in line with Tobruk, the theory was that the Tobruk garrison which we'd then relieved with fresh troops, they would break out with their tanks and push on easily towards Tripoli. That was the theory, but then we hadn't heard about the German 88mm guns.

The water in Tobruk harbour was absolutely clear, and as

you went in and out you could see this Hawker Hurricane lying on the bottom. The besiegers were only three miles outside Tobruk – when we were going out on an antisubmarine sweep they'd be shelling us! So for six months we were bombed and Christ knows what, running from Mersa Matruh to Tobruk, escorting tank landing craft.

The first time we went up there we had nothing of our own, no cigarettes or soap or anything like that, and Ramsay said had I any ideas? I said yes, we haven't got a canteen on board, because unless you were a destroyer you didn't have a canteen, so I said if you want us to run a canteen we'll do so. So I put it to the crew and with all due respect to the English, you ask them for money and they think you're a crook! They didn't want to know. So I said well, if you don't want to know I'll run it with my own money and whatever profit I make is mine.

So we came into Alex for a boiler clean, and while we were having all our alterations done I got them to put up cupboards in the storeroom on the *Wolborough* to take these goods.

The first time I think I had about £20–25 worth of stores. We had it fairly easy, we weren't bombed or anything. At Tobruk these two Aussies came aboard and they said to one of my mates 'Have you got a canteen on board, sport?' And he said 'Yeah, go down aft and see Cookie!' That was me. They called me 'Cookie'. So these two Aussies came along, asked me what I had; as I say, I only had £25 worth of stuff on board. They looked at it, they said 'All right, we'll give you fifty quid for it!' I'd doubled my money!

So we go back to Alex., and I'd doubled my money, so I doubled the amount of stores. By the time we were ready to leave Tobruk the Aussies had come back and given me their orders! I had an order book! You wouldn't believe it, would you? The money I used to earn at Tobruk I used to take ashore in Alex. and bank. The third time I did a deal with the NAAFI manager. He gave me £400 worth of stores on tick, which I'd take up to Tobruk, and then we'd share the profit. That particular night we were half way to Tobruk when this Dornier spotted us and came in low. He kept coming at us, then he'd circle round and come in again. When that bloody plane came at us for a fifth time, dropped his bomb wide, I was on the port side with my twin Lewis, and of course he was so low I couldn't have missed him. The last we saw of him – we never actually saw him crash – there was flames coming out of his tail, but whether I downed him or not, I don't know to this day. I wasn't worried about me or the ship – I was worried about the £400 worth of goods down below, because I'd have to pay for them when I got back!

The siege of Tobruk was eventually lifted after 242 days (April to December 1941) when the garrison successfully linked up with the relieving force. The shuttle service which had served as their lifeline had cost twenty-five warships and five merchantmen sunk outright, and nine warships and four merchantmen damaged.

Then I came back to England and for two years, from 42 to 44, my title was catering instructor to the Dover Command. I had the whole of the motor torpedo boats' and the trawlers' cooks to instruct, and I used to go to sea with 'em. You see the more time I spent at sea the more money I got, because ships of destroyer size and below you got hard lyers [hard lying money]. That was a lot of money in those days on top of my pay, so I didn't want to be hanging about ashore; I used to check myself into these ships.

Four or five weeks before D-Day I was out in the Channel on one of our ships, minesweeping, when we got a signal saying an MTB was coming to pick me up, take me back to Dover. I thought, what have I done now! So I get back to Dover and the officer in charge said 'You'd better put your best bib on, a car's coming for you from the Castle – the Admiral wants to see you at six o'clock this evening.' So of course what have I done? I go up to the Castle and I meet the Admiral's Secretary, who's a full-blown four ring Captain. 'Ah', he said, 'so you're the one we're waiting for!' They'd got all my papers. They knew I'd worked at the Park Lane and Grosvenor House. He said 'Now, before you meet the Admiral I'm going to tell you what it's all about. GOC Southern Command gave a banquet for senior officers some weeks ago, and the Navy wants to go one better.' I'm not telling you a word of a lie, this is the gospel truth. Bloody rationing as tight as you could have it, four weeks before D-Day, and the Navy wants to go one better. He said 'You can take who you like from Dover Command, I've got all their papers' – where they'd worked in the West End, cooks and stewards – 'take 'em over and commandeer the kitchens of a hotel in the town! Oh, and you can sign for anything!'

Would you believe that things like that went on?

6

HOSTILITIES ONLY

War required huge numbers of additional sailors, over and above what could be provided by the various reserves. This shortfall was made good by civilians conscripted for the duration of the war, known in the Navy as 'Hostilities Only' ratings, or HOs. They included many thousands of young men, sometimes enthusiastic and sometimes reluctant. But the Navy could not have fought the war without them.

Some of the conscripts came from responsible positions in civilian life – men who were middle class by upbringing and income. Many more were trades unionist by inclination. The Navy found knowing how to deal with them quite hard, and at first the tendency was to treat them no differently to the regular sailors on the lower deck. They were expected to obey orders unthinkingly and were subjected to the full rigour of naval discipline. This was unacceptable to many of these men, and much conflict and some bitterness ensued, until the process of war and the pressures of social change made the Navy more sensitive in its attitude towards its temporary sailors.

Eric Hancock was an HO. Unlike many HO sailors who were given no option as to which service they joined, but were sent to the Navy because at the moment they were called up it happened to need recruits more urgently than the other two services, he was given a choice.

I always loved the water. I'm born under Pisces; I loved swimming, lived in the water. Another thought went through my mind – I didn't relish marching everywhere on foot like soldiers had to, I'd rather be carried by a ship. But I wasn't given any choice what I would do in the RN – I went to HMS *Impregnable*, the signals school. People in civilian life didn't swear before the war, but in *Impregnable* they did! I think what instigates it is when you're at sea, in the winter in rough weather, everything is an effort – to go from here to there. The ship's tossing, you've to hang on, and you don't do it silently. You call that ship everything under the sun because it's trying to kill you, trying to wash you overboard. You're hanging on for grim death, so you swear, that's what I put it down to.

Did the danger make people superstitious?

MRS HANCOCK: Your mother used to say you were lucky, didn't she, because of the way you were born. She said they never drown . . .

ERIC: I was born in a caul – I never actually saw it, but when I joined the Navy my mother gave it me, in a sealed envelope. It was kept in my kit the whole time I was in the Navy until I lost everything. I never mentioned it to a soul but I always thought that the ship I was on was lucky, we'd never sink, because of it. All these other chaps, they don't know it, but they're on a lucky ship!

They were a very mixed group – a Geordie from Newcastle, biscuit manufacturer's rep, diplomat's son – we came from all walks of life, various parts of the country.

Like most Hostilities Only ratings, viewing the Navy through outsiders' eyes, he found many of its practices archaic. Yet it still attracted his enthusiasm and loyalty.

The barracks were terrific Victorian buildings, mess tables all the way down, old fashioned fireplace at each end, with an open fire in the winter. Great iron girders, every two feet there was a hook, that's where you slung your hammock, so you were literally touching one another. If you didn't sling your hammock before you went ashore at night you wasn't certain of getting a space when you came back, that's how cramped and full they were. Very draughty places, no comfort whatsoever, all the windows blacked out. You never saw daylight, lights on continually. Washing facilities down in the basement – rows and rows of wash basins and baths, no doors of course. It was like everything else – you had to adapt yourself, get up ten minutes earlier than everyone else and dash down there to get a sink, but if you waited ... [laughs]. No modern comforts whatsoever.

To do your washing you went across to another building, great troughs where you scrubbed and washed your stuff.

Did you like the uniform?

Well, er, yes, but it wasn't a comfortable uniform. When you joined up, everything that was issued was called 'Pusser's', and it was baggy. A sailor's No.1 suit was never from the Navy, he'd have a private tailor make it. In all these naval towns there used to be several tailors. You had an account with them and so much of your money was stopped. These tailors, when you came in from sea, they'd be one of the first chaps on board, hoping to take some orders for suits.

When you had a suit made, they would make it fit tightly, tight arms, extra wide bell bottoms – that was your 'tiddly' suit. And if it was a bit far beyond regulation, you wouldn't get ashore in it when you lined up to be inspected. The sailor in wartime was very tiddly and smart on the whole.

In wartime the name bands on our caps were never the name of the ship, and if you see a photo of a sailor taken then you'll see that his tiddly bow is over his right eye. Regulations in the Navy said it should be over your ear, but wartime it'll be over his eye. Just one of those little things that made him look that much smarter. You used to pay a chap to tie that little bow, butterfly bow. He was an expert at tying it.

You got all sorts of things in the Navy like that. You had a tailor in the barracks, operated a sewing machine – you could take any tailoring job down to him, he'd do it for you at a cost. You had dhobey firms, chaps who'd do your washing. And people would roll your tobacco – you had an issue of two tins of tobacco once a month. You could take it down to one of these chaps, and he tailor-made cigarettes for you.

The pay you received was enough to cover this?

Oh yes. On destroyers you got hard lying money, that lifted it a bit. And of course once you went to sea you wasn't spending. When you came back and went up to the pay block and he gave you sixteen quid, you wondered where it came from! You were a little millionaire going out – everyone was happy!

You prepared your own food, the only thing the cooks did was put it in the oven. The Admiralty allowed you so much a day to live on. If you overspent you had to make good. If you underspent you had the money. It's a funny idea, but that's how it worked. You had a bill at the end of the month. Sometimes we had to pay out, sometimes we had some left over – it depended where you were. Sometimes you was in places you couldn't get food. If you went abroad or called in at places, you would take the first opportunity to get fresh fruit and vegetables.

We learned the naval slang. The supplies officer always had a rating as his assistant, and his name was Jack Dusty. Jimmy, or Jimmy the One, was the First Lieutenant. Bootnecks were Royal Marines. When you join the Navy what with all the naval terms which go back for centuries, if you're a civilian you don't know whether you're coming or going.

I had the job of collecting the rum ration. I used to go in with this old three badge chap. You took an earthenware jug in a wicker basket, and at eleven o'clock it was up spirits. You'd hear the old Royal Marine sound over the loud speakers. I used to go over to the spirit room and get in the queue, and the officer would stand there – the smell when this room was unlocked, you were nearly drunk on it. The chap with the book would say so many tots, and it was measured out in beautiful polished copper measures. Then it was sealed with sealing wax, and an anchor stamp put in a seal on the top.

One particular time I thought crumbs! Feels a bit light, don't seem to have the right quantity here. I took it back to the mess, and when they opened it to issue it out it was quite a number of tots short. They sent me back with a Leading Seaman, had to go and get an officer, spirit room had to be unlocked, quite a palaver. They more or less said I'd drunk it on the way back, but of course being brand new, only in the Navy a few weeks, it got sorted out in the end. But there was a hell of a business over it. To deprive anyone of a tot in the Navy! Some people would do anything for a tot. I would at sea. It settled me. It was worth its weight in gold. Yet another chap would have his tot and bring it up immediately.

In barracks it's drawn up in the drill hall every day, or was. Huge barrels, and the rings round the barrels polished every day, brass, 'God save the King' inscription, been there for donkey's years. You can imagine the amount drawn every day in barracks because there was roughly 10,000 chaps there, and they always had to put a certain amount in extra for spillages. So when they'd finished there'd be a considerable quantity left over. That had to be tipped down the drain in front of the officer before he left, but I have heard say some officers would turn a blind eye. The old saying was that all the drains were kept highly polished – there was always a matelot on the end waiting to catch it!

Scapa was pretty grim, just a canteen there. You got your big battleships kept up there because the Germans had big ships in Norway. They would be swinging round the buoy for months. Destroyers used to be almost constantly at sea, and they used to shout at these big ships 'Why don't you go to sea!' Laugh? We'd be going out to sea and passing a battleship, and it's naval practice that you stand to attention and face the senior ship. Everything's quiet, and all of a sudden a matelot would shout 'Go to sea you bastards!' to the embarassment of everyone.

As the reservists had found before them, the newcomers – and the alien influences they brought with them – were not at first welcomed by the tightly-knit community of the RN's regulars. *George Sear* remembers the problem.

Trigger they used to call me. Because on every gun you've got a trigger sear – when you put a round up the spout, the sear retains the trigger until you fire it.

The ship I joined, *Kingston*, they were all peacetime sailors – one, two or three badge men, that had been in the Navy for eight, ten, fifteen, twenty years. And they hated the sight of us! But at the end of the war they couldn't pay a high enough tribute to chaps who'd had to do the same job as them. We had to learn it from scratch, and it wasn't a matter of even giving you weeks. I went to Shotley barracks, eight weeks training, one weekend's leave, drafted down to Pompey [Portsmouth] and off I was, out to the Red Sea.

The *Kingston*, one of the Navy's eight modern 'K' class destroyers, was soon to be involved in the nightmare battles around Crete.

I joined her in April 1941, when they were shipping troops over from the Western Desert to defend Greece. We took convoy after convoy of troops, tanks, guns and supplies over, and three days after our last trip we had to go back and start evacuating them all. They had to leave a whole damn lot behind. We got 'em to Crete, and then they really gave us a plastering. Churchill in as many words said to the Navy 'Hold Crete even if you lose the whole Eastern Mediterranean Fleet', and we virtually did.

Us and the *Kandahar*, we were two of very few destroyers in our flotilla that lasted the whole action, because some of them got damaged and had to go back, but we went right through. Greece to Crete and Crete back to Alex. Had to refuel, take on ammunition and provisions, and go up there again, by which time the Germans had Stukas in Greece waiting for us.

We were patrolling Crete because we knew they were massing all this invasion shipping in Greek ports. These 'J's and 'K's – they were all completed in 1938–39 – they were designed as fleet destroyers, primarily for surface action, against an enemy battle fleet. Their guns were low angle, so all we could do was fire at oncoming low-level bombers. High-level bombers, like Stukas, we hadn't got a chance of hitting – we could only open up with our pom-poms and small arms when they got near enough to the ship.

We lost the *Juno*; she went in a minute and a half. Just a patch of oil and debris on the water. Most blokes, peacetime an' all, it was the first time they'd seen anything like it. She was just steaming across our bows dodging the Stuka attacks as we were turning and weaving. How we got out of it I don't know, but us and the *Kandahar* got away with it.

The cruisers *Gloucester* and *Fiji* were sent to help us because we had about three hundred soldiers on board we'd picked up in Crete the previous night, plus we had some *Juno* survivors on board – fifteen; five of them died, poor devils. So the C.-in-C. despatched the *Gloucester* and *Fiji* to cover us, pick up survivors, and if necessary go into Crete under cover of darkness and pick up any more troops they could find. Of course directly the *Gloucester* steamed within sight of us she must have got a stick of bombs. She burst into flames and started sinking. The *Fiji* was plastered all day long and dodged them all, then at about six o'clock in the evening a bomb blew her boiler room open and she started to turn over. We steamed towards her, but her Captain signalled for us to turn away and save ourselves, and come back later under cover of night. This was about six, half past six in the evening, just getting dusk. We came back about half past eight and they were all bobbing about – some of them had little red lamps on their life jackets. Of course they let up a cheer. *Fiji* had 241 killed, and we saved 534. We were in a sinking condition ourselves then, all our plates were loose, rivets popping out all over; we were out of ammunition, out of food. I hadn't been down in my mess for seven days and nights. On the guns we were living on biscuits, cocoa and corned beef. The ship was full up, overloaded. We were told to return to Alex – the signal said we should reprovision and come back, though we weren't in any fit state to. So afterwards we went back up there again, trying to pick survivors off Crete, until the powers that be realized that it was useless. We just had to abandon it.

Did you feel that you were a lucky ship?

Oh, definitely. They all said that. First thing we say when we get round the table at a reunion, how we got through Crete! How we survived! And the near misses we had on every operation we went on. We were what they called the 'gash boat' of the flotilla – the junior boat. Our Skipper was the junior Lieutenant-Commander. The flotilla leader had a four ring Captain – ours was Captain Mack, marvellous bloke he was – the half leader had a Commander, three rings, and all the other destroyer Skippers were two and a half rings, Lieutenant-Commanders. Had he not been killed later, our Skipper with the record he'd got would have either gone to a bigger ship or become half leader of another flotilla, we wouldn't have kept him. But the whole of our career with the Mediterranean Fleet we were the junior boat, which meant that in harbour we'd have to go to what we called the gash boat buoy – not all the destroyers could tie up alongside, so it was always us who got the buoy.

Sometimes even the most unlikely conscript brought with him unusual skills – if the Navy took the time to discover his real potential.

Alan Wilson, brought up in Singapore, appeared on the surface to be the proverbial 'square peg in a round hole'.

Reporting to Skegness was a bit of a culture shock, as you can imagine. I'd never heard a four-letter obscenity in so many different accents up until that time! It was freezing cold, and we went through the business of induction, squarebashing, inoculations – I had to spend three days and two nights in my uniform because my arm swelled up so much I couldn't get out of it! And then in the way of things they just simply allocated us to being one thing or another. Because I wore glasses I became Ordinary Telegraphist Wilson, and they sent me to – I can't even remember where now – to try to learn to be a telegraphist.

Well, they failed abysmally. I hadn't the faintest idea *why* I couldn't learn morse code, but they opted me out. I next went to Wetherby in Yorkshire, where I spent the next part of the winter building an assault course which was going to be for training commando types. That was truly exhausting, and at the end of that time, still not having a trade as it were, I went to a training establishment at Aberdeen. There I became a Petty Officers' mess man – they couldn't find anything else I could do.

Looking after five or six POs was quite interesting – you got a different view on life from what you got in your own mess. And then at some point, and I cannot really remember exactly when, somebody said 'But what can you actually *do*?' It was apparent that I had been reasonably well educated, and I spoke quite nicely and all the rest of it, but the only thing I could think of that I could do was speak Malay. This was my second language, because of my childhood. So I said this, and the next thing I got was a chit to come down to London and go and see Captain somebody-or-other at the Admiralty. This was my first experience of a high-ranking officer, because he was a four ringer. He gave me about a five minute interview and – I remember it very clearly – he made me repeat some Malay, then he handed me a square of paper with a Chinese character on it and asked me to copy it, and so I did that. And then I went back to Aberdeen. That was the beginning of a period of Limbo.

Ultimately they suddenly drafted me again, and I was told to report to the School of Oriental and African Studies in London to begin learning Japanese. I was given ten weeks with thirty other chaps to learn spoken Japanese of a fairly primitive nature – you know, 'Angels one-five' type operational Japanese. If you consistently got 80 per cent in the examinations, and 90 per cent in the last two, you passed the course. Actually I lost about ten pounds during that course, but I did it none the less.

The next things were concerning fitting oneself to do this job, which was essentially going wherever the Japanese happened to be, listening to them on the radio, and acting accordingly. Since this might involve all sorts of funny things like raiding parties and so on, we went to a couple of places to learn some quite unpleasant tricks of one sort or another. We learned how to hump our radios around and put them up in the jungle, and so on. And then we went for weapons training at Whale Island, Portsmouth.

From there we went out to Calcutta, where we sat and listened to real Japanese as spoken on the ground. Then having done that for a little while we went to Ceylon, and whenever the fleet went out, we went too.

You had background knowledge about what the Japanese ground-air radio was doing, so you got up rather early in the morning and you sat for the whole day until sundown, listening up and down the radio scale. Of course you picked up a lot of stuff that was totally irrelevant, but periodically you caught something that concerned you, whereupon you – well, as I did once, turned the entire fleet around and had it going the other way. We went to sea in carriers, battleships, cruisers, the lot. It was a very wide experience. I recall going out with the *Richelieu*, the French battleship – fine ship.

And your job on these ships was to listen in to the Japanese frequencies and report what was happening?

I suppose by and large you could say that the important area would be the Burma-Penang-Andaman Islands triangle. If they were patrolling that, then everything coming in and out of the Straits would be visible to them. In fact on one occasion I was listening in and I heard this fellow actually counting out the ships – he said 'I can see one battleship, two cruisers . . .' and so on. It was that sort of thing that the Admiral wanted to know, naturally. Plus were they running their patrols regularly? Had they seen us? Did they expect us? All that sort of thing.

We were in a number of actions of one sort or another, then when each operation was over we'd go back and sit in Colombo waiting for the next one. The most exciting time came, I suppose, during the build-up to Operation Zipper, which was going to be launched from India to retake Burma, but which was pre-empted by the atom bombs and turned into the re-occupation of the entire area from Burma to our side of New Guinea.

We sailed into Penang harbour and sat there at anchor while General Itagaki and Admiral Fukudome argued over whether or not to sign the surrender document for South East Asia. Itagaki had wanted to go on fighting, but the Admiral, Fukudome, said no, the Emperor says to give up.

HOs also proved capable of handling even the newest and most sophisticated of the Navy's equipment. *Dick McCreedy* was trained as an operator on shipboard radar, which was then in its infancy.

When the war started I was only sixteen. I was one of a family of eight, and I was one of the youngest. 'Oh, you won't go in the war', my father said, 'It'll all be over by then'. But I was the first one to be called up! [laughs] – the others were tradesmen in reserved occupations. I was called up in October 1942. Looking back I wouldn't have missed it for the world, but at the time nobody liked it, either the war itself or being in the Navy. I wasn't worried about it from what I can remember – at that age you're not worried.

I went to Portsmouth, HMS *Collingwood*, for training. Keep fit and marching, rope work, climbing up ladders, getting thrown in water, things like that. Getting you all to work together. Everybody's the same, when they first start; you must have that basic grounding. Then on the notice board were these various jobs, submarines or whatever, and on there was radar, RDF. What's that job? Oh, it's not bad – not a bad little number. Something to do apart from just swabbing decks. So I put in for radar, and all of a sudden it was you, you and you – Isle of Man.

There was a hill there called Onchan Head, and everyone went there to train on all the latest radar equipment. The Navy had taken over the town, all these big restaurants and shops on the front at Douglas, and billeted us in the houses. Further along were German POWs.

We learned all about these radar sets – never seen anything like them before in our lives – then they gave us tests, so many marks, we passed out and we came back to HMS *Victory*, Portsmouth, to wait for a draft.

I was allocated to HMS *Crane*, a brand new sloop built at Dumbarton. I can see it now, long way to go there, beautiful, smell of new paint – I think they were still painting it actually. They really wanted them in a hurry, to fight the U-boats. We did our trials in the Scottish islands and all round the coast, based at Greenock, and then we were ready for operations. I think there were about ten or twelve in our mess, and we had one senior hand looking after us.

Life on board, as with all small ships, was far from comfortable. The new sailors simply had to adjust to it.

We slept in hammocks at first, but in the North Atlantic the ship would be going over so far with the sea that we were hitting the ceiling, and if anything happened we knew we'd never get out, so we took to sleeping on or under the mess tables, with our life belts on.

Were you able to sleep under those conditions?

Oh yes. You had to really. Since I was on radar, of course once you leave harbour you're on call all the time, looking out for things. We had three different sets on board. One was a gunnery set for gun ranging, instead of manual rangefinders; then there was a long range set which was on top of the mast, to pick up planes a long way off; and there was this very low beam set, which was the latest one. That could pick up surfaced submarines.

Four-hour watches, two of us – you was in twos – in very small cubicles no more than three feet square at the most. And dark. Door shut, with big blackout curtains at night – and I wasn't a very good sailor in those days. I kept a bucket for if it was bad! But usually after the first day or two I'd be all right. The ship could do what it liked, go anywhere, because my stomach had settled. Sometimes the aerial would jam, which always happened in the middle of the night, so one of you had to go out, up the mast and free the aerial. All in a night's work! Eight till twelve, twelve till four, four till eight, and so on.

At action stations two of you manned the gunnery one, bearing and range, though fortunately we never had to use it in action, only on tests. But the submarine one we did use most of the time, especially at night in convoys.

What did you think of the Captain?

Very good, calm, although we didn't have a lot to do with him because there was so much going on. We thought he was old – he was probably only about thirty-five! But then we was all just boys then.

Was discipline tight?

No. On a small ship it was very good. You'd wear overalls. Do your own thing. As long as you done your job, you was as right as rain. Discipline in the Navy is strict anyway, but the bigger ships were like floating barracks.

Most of the ship's company were HOs. The old boys were in charge – the Petty Officers were regulars. But not all the officers; the senior ones were, but the junior officers were only like us really. All the radar men were in just for the war.

Were your family happy about you being in the Navy?

When I registered, in 1941, at that time it was a bit dodgy. The Navy was going through a bad patch; a lot of ships were being sunk. But once I got in it picked up. Two of my brothers were in the Army, and I would say I had a better war than them. The Navy was the best, you see the world for nothing!

But people were still anxious to return to civilian life – at the end of the war?

Yes, they wanted to get out. They'd had enough, most of them. Every day they'd look up the notice board, their age and service group.

Arthur Watson also felt that small ships were infinitely preferable to large ones, after sampling life in one of the smallest units of the fleet.

I arrived at midday, to find what I at first thought was a motor gun boat tied to the jetty in Portland harbour. There were only two crew members aboard – 'Texas' Holt, an AB, helped me through the hatch. He told me about the discipline expected from the Coxswain, what the other members of the crew were like, and of course the Skipper and Jimmy the One. I thought I could cope. Officers' rounds that evening gave me a fleeting glimpse of Number One, then a good look at the night order book. An entry in this referred to me as an 'extra Ordinary Seaman'. Everyone thought this was highly amusing, of course; I did just wonder then, and even some times after, whether I was extraordinary!

In fact our job was to tow a floating object, mostly like twin paravanes with a flag above. The idea was for us to meet a convoy returning home and give the gunners some target practice. Well, you may think that they had enough target practice without our help, but there was a good reason for more. Apparently, when engaged with the enemy no one could really tell just how good, or bad, our gunners were. So we met them, they fired, we registered the shots and recorded them.

One of my duties included being cook for a period of three months – nobody else wanted the job. Another was acting as buoy jumper. I couldn't swim, thus ensuring I would be more careful leaping on and off of huge tossing iron drums in stormy seas. A third was that I should have a canvas bag full of wooden pegs or dowels, sizes to fit shell or bullet holes, and a mallet to hammer them home. I thought at first this was a joke. No, it was serious.

Well, I began to master the art of cooking in cramped conditions, with an oven the size of a biscuit tin and three burners on top heated by a primus stove. Accidents of a minor type were frequent. One incident I remember with amusement now happened one morning as we were leaving harbour. I had prepared the vegetables and placed a rice pudding and a meat pie in the oven, so I informed the Coxswain that everything was cooking in the galley and was told to secure everything before we left harbour. I tied the saucepans to the little rail round the stove, then tied the lids on with line. We all stood on deck as usual, supposedly at attention, as we left – facing the flag at the harbour entrance. 'Swain said I should make sure everything was safe in the galley as soon as possible. We hit the rough the moment I went below. The saucepans were dangling on their strings, the contents, by some miracle, had spilled into a bucket of dhobeying. The cabbage was rewashed and back into the pot, likewise the potatoes. I rinsed the dhobeying out and replaced it in the bucket! Nobody complained about the meal – most of the lads said it was good, preferable to corned beef sandwiches. By the way, I forgot to mention that the meat pie had spilled over into the rice pudding, so I put the rice pudding on the top shelf of the oven, and some of that then spilled over into the pie. Even so it was all eaten, and no one seemed to complain.

To tie up in harbour, my duty was to stand on the bows with a heaving line ready in hand. Approaching the huge bucking bronco of a buoy, looking for the right moment to jump, was nerve-racking. Jimmy the One said 'Jump!' I paused for a second longer, then leapt onto the small, heaving platform. I passed the line through the heavy ring and threw the line back on board. Next I pulled the bowline through the ring, all the while keeping my balance. Once we were tied up I had to scramble back aboard. Jimmy the One was annoyed because I hadn't jumped when he gave the order. I explained it was difficult to time the jump from where he stood, and he grudgingly conceded that I could be right, so from then on it was up to me. Iron ladders were another hazard, more so when covered in seaweed. Some ladders I swear were more than twenty feet high. It was one step up, two down sometimes, when there was no one to catch a heaving line on the jetty. I think I made a good jumper, because I never missed!

The cold was always a big handicap, as every matelot knows.

Designed during the First World War
and lost during the Second. The graceful battlecruiser HMS *Hood*

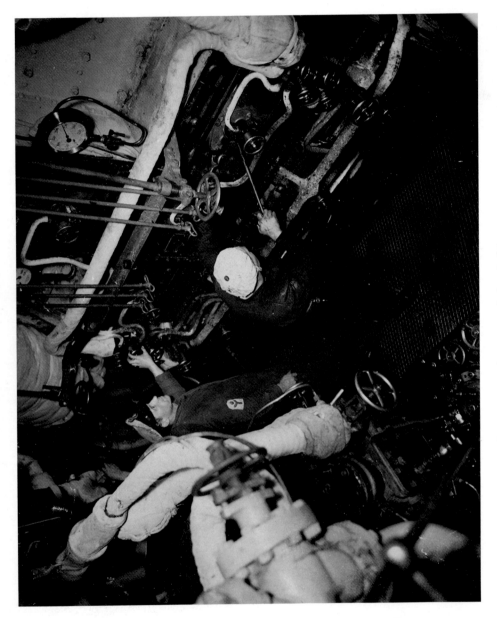

Boiler room of a battleship

Destroyer deck in heavy weather

Lookout on board HMS *Suffolk* surveys the ice floes of the Denmark Strait

Spectacular explosion of the US ammunition ship *Mary Luckenbach*,
taken from the flight deck of the escort carrier HMS *Avenger*

Replacing the losses.
A cargo ship and tanker in the fitting out basin

Dockyard matey at work on the screw of a cruiser

Shell room of a destroyer.
Loading up the hoist with four more rounds.

Double-decker bus converted for use in training Merchant Navy gunners

Packed hangar deck of a carrier

'Batsman' and Swordfish during a deck landing

Control room of a submarine

Wrens at the rifle range,
with a Royal Marines instructor

Carrier HMS *Ark Royal* capsizing off Gibraltar,

One cold autumn afternoon we set sail to give a convoy a good shot at our target. We sailed for some hours to and fro, then the convoy drifted out of sight. I sat on a little ledge on the port side of the wheelhouse, with the handle of the speed indication telegraph at my right shoulder. Suddenly there was a distant volley of shots, not an unfamiliar sound to us. But then another volley shattered the wheelhouse. A low moaning voice came down the voice pipe, 'Stop engines'. I stopped engines. Then the Skipper's voice, 'Start engines, full speed all three!' Again I obeyed the command. We shuddered forward against the heavy sea. The Skipper again: 'Get up here, Watson!' I went on deck for'ard and helped Pogson to drag 'Swain from the bridge. It was obvious he had taken at least five small shells. We covered him with a blanket and left him on the forecastle. Meanwhile we were at full speed heading away from our adversary. Jimmy the One had suffered an injury to his leg. The Skipper had a gash on his head. As we drew nearer to Portsmouth harbour in the dark they warned us 'Send correct signal or turn about'. Ship to shore signals changed at certain times of the day, and the code book was missing among the debris. Portsmouth was not our home base, of course, but we happened to be nearer Portsmouth than Portland. Someone dashed below to find a torch. Sparks searched among the debris for the code book. Another signal from the shore, 'Identify!' We tried to send morse with the torch, but this didn't satisfy anyone on the harbour defences, and a searchlight played full on us. Sparks found a means of sending the right signal by semaphore just as a voice boomed out 'We shall count to three and then open fire!'. Then we heaved a sigh of relief as we were given the go-ahead.

Next day we cleaned up a bit, but it was curtains for the boat. A couple of days later most of us were busy carrying stores aboard *MGB.59*. There was Taff, Poggy, Fairy, Guns, Mac, Stokes, but not 'Swain of course, and Sparks was going for another higher course. No Skipper and no Jimmy. Our new Sparks was called Rattler, Rattler Morgan. Rattler always seemed to win at uckers [a shipboard game similar to ludo] at sixpence per game! We got along like a house on fire, but then so did the rest of the crew. Being cramped up in such a small boat was a bit claustrophobic at times, but I can't remember a time when we lost our tempers.

We were now based at Portsmouth, at the end of the jetty near the Wrens' quarters. There were several huts for training facilities, and a single large mess hut, where we sometimes sat with the shore-based ratings. One of these, a huge six-foot-three-in-his-socks AB called Lofty Parks, decided we weren't entitled to. I foolishly challenged him to settle our differences outside. We never reached outside – I opened the door and he hit me in the left eye. His right hand had a huge ring on the finger which split open my eye. I retaliated with a punch on his huge ugly nose, then he rushed at me and pushed me onto a trestle table, which collapsed. The contents – potatoes, gravy, treacle pudding – covered the pair of us as we wrestled on the floor. Lofty seemed to have a most vile temper. I felt sure he intended to kill me, as he put his huge hands round my throat and squeezed. I kicked out and wriggled to free myself, but he hung on relentlessly. Then half a dozen lads lifted off the table and pulled us apart. My eye needed two stitches. We had to pay for the breakages, and only got off a charge because we both said it was an accident.

For my part I felt hurt; my pride had been squashed, and I felt I had let down my shipmates by not putting up a better show. So I bought a punch ball on elastic and fitted it up in the tiny mess space on board *MGB.59* – every spare moment I would hook up this ball and thrash the daylights out of it. I told the lads I'd challenge Lofty to a boxing match, in the proper naval tradition. Someone, I'll never know who, must have had enough of my thumping away every five minutes, because I found the ball slashed to pieces one day. I remember accusing everyone, but no one would admit to being the culprit.

We travelled around quite a lot with our little boat, and found a temporary base in Weymouth. It was at Weymouth that I got a chance to try my hand at swimming. With the aid of a scrambling net and a round lifebuoy I felt a lot braver, but even so I never gained enough confidence to lark about in the water and enjoy it as did most of them. We carried on with our usual job of towing a target, or helping experiment with new innovations. One night, unfortunately, some nervous gunner used us for a target instead of the contraption we were towing. This may have been because the target had been nearly destroyed. I don't really know the details, but then we hardly ever did in those days. So the shells tore through halliards and the mast and rigging. The Skipper ordered hard-a-starboard and we headed straight for the culprit, shining a light onto our White Ensign. The Skipper shouted through his loudhailer 'What do you think that is?' No one was hurt, by some miracle, and we steamed off back to base.

For a while after that things seemed a bit slow. Then we were ordered to pack steaming bags, or overnight kit. The whole crew then boarded a train for Felixstowe. Here, up on chocks, was an old MTB. Our orders were to get her ready for sea. She was pulled off the chocks into the creek, and within two and a half days we sailed her round to Portsmouth – no armament, no munitions and not much confidence in her seaworthiness! This was just the beginning of a career in salvage for us. We made quite a few trips to all parts of the coast rescuing old craft. This, though we didn't know it, was in preparation for D-Day.

Everyone put forward ideas of what was going on. A few wild rumours spread around! Inevitably the day came, and we took on more stores and ammunition onto *MGB.59*, plus two more ABs, and set sail in rough weather on the night of 5/6 June 1944 under orders to stick rigidly to a convoy of assorted ships. Normally we'd circle round a convoy, to keep our engines running at a comfortable speed. We did our job very well through the night, but at the expense of our motors which were becoming sluggish. Through the night all was quiet, until we reached the coast of France.

Huge plumes of flame and smoke covered a large area of the shoreline. Alongside us, too close for comfort, a rocket-firing vessel loosed its rockets onto the beach – the explosion nearly lifted us out of the water. Then another salvo of rockets blasted a hole in the cliffs, leaving a steep incline up to a wooded patch. I could just make out this picture in the split second before it was pitch black again. Then we stopped engines. Mac came up on the bridge to report that the couplings had broken, so there we were in the middle of it all, helpless. We drifted nearer to shore then dropped anchor. Shells passed over us for the rest of the night, planes droned over constantly and landing craft sailed past, too busy to tend to our plight. In the morning the wind grew stronger, and in the afternoon she began dragging her anchor. We couldn't lift it, and our bows were being pulled down into the sea, so we had to release the anchor by slipping the chain. We shot off like a cork. There were so many vessels around, but we found it difficult if not impossible to get a line onto any of them. Then at last we managed to tie up to a sunken wreck. We lasted there for two hours, fending off all the while, but the gale became so fierce that our lines parted leaving the Samson Post [*small derrick mast on a cargo ship*] with two fingers sticking up like Mr Churchill's victory sign. Every one of us was on the lookout for hazards – driftwood, rocks, smashed dinghies, and other small craft. Somehow we warded off all of them. Darkness fell again, which made things worse. Sparks was now trying to get help, but the reply was 'No assistance available.'

At last the storm abated, and we rested peacefully for a few hours tied to another wreck and managed to get some food. There was no water left for washing – we could use salt water, of course, but this always left a sticky feeling. Then it rained. All of us had the same idea – off overalls, up top, lather up and let the rain wash it off. It promptly stopped raining.

Next day some of us rowed the Skipper ashore. I found out later the place was called Bernieres-sur-Mer, and the landing area was called Juno. Then a colossal US tug agreed to tow us back to Portsmouth. By the time we had taken aboard a 4 inch hawser night was upon us again. The Yanks made one proviso – if we should meet any E-boats lurking in the open waters our line would be cut and we would be on our own. We agreed, and away we went. Following in the wake of the tug was bad enough, but steering in those conditions was really tiring – I took over at the wheel when 'Swain had had enough twisting the wheel from port to starboard and back for a solid hour. Rattler started singing, and we all sang through the night until we reached Portsmouth.

A short while after this they – that is, the Admiralty – asked for volunteers to go to Australia. We all thought it would be great. It was arranged for the whole of our crew to go out to start a flotilla. I don't think any of us realized what it would be like fighting the Japanese. We sailed aboard the *Mauretania* as passengers, and this is when I again ran into Lofty Parks. He was given a duty as POs mess man, and so was I! He could not have been friendlier! Strange as it may seem, I quickly found him to be a great oppo!

The Navy quickly realized the necessity of picking out potential officers from among the flood of new recruits, and encouraged men it felt would be suited to holding commissioned rank, like *Allan Burke*.

There was an AFO, an Admiralty Fleet Order, which as far as I can remember said people who had had a university education were invited to put their names forward. I didn't bother, although I'd done one year at Manchester University before I went into my father's business. But one day my Deputy Divisional Commander suddenly said 'Your name Burke?' I said yes. He said 'Why don't you apply for a commission?' I looked at him in astonishment. 'Well', he said, 'every week there's marks given to us, in gunnery, signalling, anchor work, the whole thing, and you've come top week after week in every subject; so I've arranged for you to see the Captain of the base on Sunday after divisions.' I went along and he interviewed me, and I was recommended. The idea was that you went as a CW candidate aboard your first ship, which in my case was one of the old 'V&W' class destroyers, and that started it. After that we went down, three of us, to Portsmouth for an interview with a board. The results were pinned up the next day, and those who passed were sent to Lancing College, HMS *King Alfred*, to do an initial course of three months.

What was the interview with the board like?

There was a sort of semicircular table behind which they were sitting, gold braid up to their elbows, and there was a highly polished floor and an armchair. You walked across fearful that you were going to skid on this floor. I wondered how I should sit – should I sit nonchalantly, or what? They asked all sorts of questions – some elementary mathematical questions which really didn't matter, and they asked about religion and sport. Why they said that I don't know. And what ship did I serve in, and how did I like it. And I always remember at the end they said 'Well, if we recommend you, what would you like to serve in?' I said 'Well, I'd like to go back to the Atlantic.' They thought I was mad! They said 'You'd like to go back to the Western Approaches? Why? Haven't you had enough?' I said I believed that's where the war was going to be won. It was fairly nerve-racking, because we were all young and awe-struck, and we'd never met such senior officers before.

Many regular officers in fact harboured deep misgivings over the prospect of being joined in the wardroom by hurredly-commissioned HOs. And when it became clear that promotion for the new men might in many cases be faster than their own, an extra dimension was added to their unease.

I always remember when I served aboard HMS *Whitehall*, that first destroyer, as a CW candidate, all the officers were regulars. One of them was very patronizing, he said 'You people will only be doing shore jobs, none of you will go to sea as officers – it's ridiculous, you can't do the job of the regulars!'

I was very bold and cocky as a young man, and I corrected him. I said 'Sir, you have the wrong idea.' I said 'The war is going to grow, the Navy's going to grow, so much it'll be impossible to man the ships with all RN officers. Who knows, any one of us here could end up as CO of a ship.' He got very indignant over this, but I know that of the three of us who passed, one ended up as a second in command, I ended up as a commanding officer, and the third went into a shore job. So he was only thirty-three per cent right!

I think there was a certain amount of jealousy if I can put it that way. He was regular RN, and we were lower deck, and I think he resented the fact that we could rise maybe above him.

When you went to sea as a rating, did it fit with what you expected?

Oh it was murderous. I've never experienced anything like it, because these were old World War One destroyers. HMS

Whitehall was one of the 'V&W' class; she was one of the last to be built, but the lower deck was appalling. There weren't enough hammock hooks to go round so you slept where you could, the messdecks were always flooded, foul-smelling and water sloshing about. I had to sleep on the messdeck table. The other ratings were all regulars. They were a pretty rough bunch, I must say, but they were all right. Pretty foul mouthed! Some of them did resent the fact that we were CW candidates – the standing joke was that when the Bosun used to come round piping lunch he used to shout 'Hands to dinner; CW candidates to lunch!' But all in all they were OK.

When you went to Lancing College, what kind of things did you learn there?

Well, it was a wide variety of subjects. Of course you were a seaman by then, you'd been serving at sea, so they didn't teach you how to take a watch, but we did gunnery, and you learned elementary navigation, boat handling, and heaven knows what. It could only be a skeleton outline of what you would experience later on. Pilotage; coastal navigation; they tried to teach you how to take sightings astronomically, but that didn't sink in with any of us, it was too complicated – it involved trigonometry, geometry and algebra; things like that, but mainly the basics of seamanship and navigation.

So this was an attenuated version of Dartmouth?

Yes, but crammed into three months. You had to really swot – even when you were doing guard duty. It left you with very little sleep. A lot of the lads, the upper echelon, aristocratic people, thought they would sail through this and they used to go up to London for the weekend. And they failed. I didn't – I really swotted, worked very hard, and my only recreation was playing a game of rugby or football on a Saturday. I never went further than Brighton for a stroll round. I realized I'd have to work hard, and I did. There were three grades of passing out certificates, first, second and third, and I was fortunate enough to get a first class certificate.

Again I was asked what I wanted to do, and I said I wanted to go back to the Western Approaches, and again they looked astonished. Because in those days the Atlantic was an absolute killing ground.

What would they have considered a prudent choice?

Oh, a big ship perhaps – aircraft carrier, battleship – or a shore job somewhere. Anyway, I went to the 8th Escort Group based in Londonderry, in Northern Ireland. My new ship was much smaller than the *Whitehall*, with a crew of about sixty, I think. I went aboard in trepidation, wondering how I would behave, and I was so naive and ignorant that instead of calling the First Lieutenant 'Number One' I called him 'Sir'. As a fellow officer you always called him 'Number One'. He barked 'Don't say "Sir", call me "Number One"!' There were only four officers on board, and I was the junior Sub. The Captain and the First Lieutenant were both the same rank, Lieutenants. It was a smaller ship and you knitted more easily together, but we were doing the same work as destroyers.

In your various ships, did you feel the Navy had the right people at the top?

No, not always. The fact is that in any service, as in industry, there's bound to be mistakes. But they did try. I don't know whether you've heard of Tobermory, the working-up base for escorts. The Admiral there, Vice Admiral Sir Gilbert Stephenson, he was a terror. He had the authority to yank any officer out and replace him, except commanding officers – they had to be appointed by the Admiralty. He used to send inspection teams aboard for sea exercises lasting three or four days, and put you through some extraordinary things, to test your initiative. I was fortunate in so much as my second ship went to Tobermory after some repairs, so when I later became First Lieutenant, second in command of a ship, and went up after a refit I knew all the tricks, which stood me in good stead.

What were your duties as First Lieutenant?

You were responsible really to the commanding officer for the discipline, training, and everything that happened on the ship. You also did your ordinary watches, the First Lieutenant's watch was from 0400 to 0800, which meant that you were ready to fall the crew in at 0900 and supervise what they were doing, give them tasks. But you did everything. There was a saying in the Navy – the First Lieutenant only goes ashore on the kedge anchor. The kedge anchor is used to pull the ship off a sandbank or something.

When you got into port, the Chief Engineer would come to you with his list of defects and requirements, the officer who was doing the administration with the Coxswain would give you a list of stores, the gunnery officer would say if there were any defects on the guns, and give you his requirements of ammunition, the antisubmarine officer would add his list of depth charges, primers, pistols and so on. And the First Lieutenant would then go up to the base and plead with tears in his eyes that the ship was falling to pieces, and he must have another day in port, and they'd say very sorry, you're sailing tomorrow. You handled it all when you received the information. And then they started storing, fuelling, taking on water and provisions, gun ammunition and depth charges.

What kind of disciplinary problems would you have to deal with?

Well, if it was, say, someone coming back on board pickled, the officer of the watch might turn a blind eye, as long as the lad got to the messdeck. But if he was urinating on the upper deck or something ridiculous he would put him on the First Lieutenant's report and he'd get a couple of days extra work, or similar punishment. The serious things you'd probably have to send them ashore for court martial, but we only had one case in all my experience.

So it was mainly relatively minor things?

Well there's grades, it's laid down in the rules and regulations, which were like the Bible. You were guided by those – how many days stoppage of pay, how many days stoppage of leave, how many hours extra work a day. It was all laid out for you.

Were you ever in action? Were you ever hit?

I got two. I was very lucky – I was on watch, and we'd been sent to look for a straggler, and the weather in the Atlantic was appalling. The cloud ceiling was I don't think more than a thousand feet; grey, dirty day. And I heard an aircraft but I couldn't see it. Our radar was hopeless, we couldn't pick it up. It sounded by the note of the engines like a Focke-Wulf Condor [a German maritime patrol aircraft], so I took no chances and rang action stations. When the Captain came on the bridge he said I'd done the right thing, and sent me aft to my gun station – I was in charge of the after guns.

And suddenly right up the wake comes a Condor. I was fortunate – he must have been running low on cannon shells, because he opened fire with his machine guns only, as a sighting burst, and I felt my leg go from under me, didn't know what it was. Then he opened up with his cannon as well, but by then he was three-quarters of the way up the ship, so he only hit the forecastle with the full blast. If he'd hit me with that he probably would have taken both my legs off. As it was, I stopped two bullets. Ruined my leather seaboots. I lost a fair amount of blood, but – touch wood – I was very, very lucky.

Did it cross your mind at any point that you might not survive the war?

Oh, quite often. But not from enemy action – from the weather. One time we were on the port beam of a convoy, and it was blowing hard. In the Atlantic it used to blow for three, four weeks at a time; mountainous seas. But the ship was riding comfortably enough, when our Sub-Lieutenant got a signal from the senior officer of the escort telling us to change our position from port beam to port quarter. Instead of telling the Captain, which he should have done immediately, and reducing speed so that we dropped back gradually into the port quarter position, he just ordered the wheel to be put over, and came broadside on to these seas! An absolutely tremendous wave hit us and heeled us over, and she lay over like a dead thing. I was in the wardroom with the Captain having a cup of coffee, and suddenly this wave heeled us over, and water was pouring in. We splashed our way out, and the Captain clung onto the ladder leading up, against the side of the ship. I grabbed at it and missed, and I was swept right along the deck. You couldn't even see the rails – they were under water, she was laying so far over – and I thought, this is it. I remember looking through a green haze; I thought I was a goner. But I clung on to the canvas cover on the depth charge thrower, and I managed to struggle across to the ladder.

We survived. It took us about twenty minutes to bring her around. We lost both boats, swept away, and there were minor injuries amongst the crew, but we got through it.

Did you get people losing their nerve?

I can only remember one case. This was at the beginning of the war when I was aboard the *Whitehall* – we got into port and Liverpool was being hammered in the raids, so we sent out a fire-fighting party. The docks were ablaze, and we were working all night with hoses, it really was an inferno. And one of our ratings disappeared.

Afterwards we all went on the quay, and the CO said – he didn't mention this lad's name, and he didn't punish him – he said 'One rating has disgraced the ship; we all know who he is', and he said 'We'll have none of that again'. That's the only time I saw cowardice.

There were cases where ratings wouldn't go down to the mess, no matter how bad the weather; they'd sleep on the upper deck, but they still did their duties. We understood that. No one said you're a coward or anything like that. Personally I was scared stiff every moment of the war. I think anyone who was at sea with the convoys, and says he wasn't frightened, is a liar. But you control it, and you remain calm, or outwardly calm, because you know panic is terribly contagious.

Yet the thing I used to hate the most was an anchor watch. Say you're in the Firth of Clyde, or Belfast Lough, and it's blowing like hell, and you're doing an officer's anchor watch. Ships all around you in the gloom. You think 'Is our anchor dragging? Shall I call the Captain out? Is that ship a bit nearer to us because she's dragging?' I used to think 'Oh God, if only we were at sea!' I used to hate anchor watches, hated them. Of course once you were CO yourself and you were called out you had to decide what to do, whether to pay out more chain, or use your engines. There was always a thousand and one things. I never used to turn in at night when I was a CO, I used to doze in an armchair, and then every half hour or so get up and wander up to the bridge, see everything was all right.

As the Navy's needs continued to grow, the logical next step was to pre-select potential candidates before they even began their training – a revised system of entry which was known as the 'Y Scheme'. *John Green* entered the Navy under its terms in 1941.

I joined under a scheme called the Y Scheme, which was aimed at graduates and ex-public school people. I was interviewed in April 1941, where I was asked to recognize various types of ship and that sort of thing – obviously I knew just enough about it to be accepted. I actually joined for training in June, and they sent me to *Collingwood*, Fareham, for three-months' basic training, integration into the Navy. You joined as a rating. The theory was that if you joined under the Y Scheme you were an instant CW candidate. You did basic training, you did so many weeks at sea, and then you came back to do your commission course. But it didn't always work out that way.

My first ship was a fleet minesweeper, HMS *Speedy*, and we did two east coast convoys and then we went to Russia. We took a PQ convoy to Russia in November 1941, then we stayed there until February 1942. *Speedy* was one of the bigger minesweepers, 884 tons, which made her more comfortable to be on than a destroyer – we were simply up and down like a cork, whereas destroyers went partly through the wave. But then obviously being that sort of size, we rolled like mad. They were some of the first small ships in the Navy where you could go from one end to the other below deck, unlike a destroyer, where you had to come up on the upper deck to get past the engine room down below. You could get from one end of the ship to the other and straight up onto the compass platform literally without getting wet. Operational strength was 115 – we had 5 officers and 110 ratings.

What was the ship's company like?

They made it quite clear that if you were an HO you weren't even fit to man the boat falls – they'd never make a seaman out of you! But eventually I think everything was welded together because quite obviously with 100 men on a small ship, they'd jolly well got to!

Did you form an impression in those early days of what the pre-war Navy had been like?

Oh yes. Very very unbending, and a little bit limited in outlook. I well remember the attack on Pearl Harbor, and later on – well, not that much later on – in the war I came to the conclusion that air power was going to be vitally important.

But the RN personnel, in all honesty, all they wanted to hear was their guns going bang.

We went to Russia the first time in November 1941. Stalin considered us only about one degree superior to the Germans; we weren't allowed to leave the ship or anything like that. And when I came back after the first trip, my mother said 'Where have you been?' I said I've been to Russia, but they didn't believe me. In my opinion the Russians were never allies, they were co-belligerents. But we'd been told how marvellous they were, and there's no doubt about it – in terms of sacrifice, they were fantastic.

So you weren't allowed ashore?

Well, there was a soldier with a machine gun, but you were allowed off to go to the Fleet Club, about twenty ratings at a time. You met Russian girls there, but if one of them even accepted a bar of chocolate you wouldn't see her again – because that was regarded as fraternizing. Stalin had this obsession with the system being tainted by influences from the West.

And they were so incredibly inefficient. We went to sea usually in twos and threes to keep the passage open, and on one occasion as we came back we took the Russian pilot on board, and after about twenty minutes, half an hour, he got very agitated. The Skipper more or less said bugger off now – we know how to get in here. So about an hour later we discovered we'd just gone over a Russian minefield, and it was so badly laid we didn't get a touch – nor did anyone else that we knew of. One of the things that is important in minesweeping is the accuracy of your navigation, because you've got to chart the waters that have been swept, and we had an RN navigating officer, which was comparatively rare for a small ship, in order to keep the charts up to date.

My particular job on *Speedy* was 'A' gun, though we couldn't actually use it because it was all frozen up. The ice had to be constantly chipped off the upper deck, because if you didn't you got dangerously top-heavy. Mind you, the Germans' guns seemed to be all right, because we were out with *Hebe* on one occasion, the visibility was awful, and suddenly there was the most enormous bang and the first shell hit us. It brought part of the topmast down, and it fell onto the whistle lanyard which went from the funnel to the bridge. Everybody rushed up onto the upper deck, but we couldn't see anything, and just then the second shell hit us. We never actually saw them. We simply cut the sweeps and that was that.

That's not bad firing on their part

That's right, they probably fired a salvo of five and they hit us with one out of the five, then once out of the second five. Why they didn't close the range I don't know. We couldn't fire anything; maybe the .50 cal. machine gun; we certainly couldn't fire our 4 inch guns.

This was your first action?

Yes. It was so quick, dead quick. Once you've got both sweeps out you've got six hundred fathoms [1,200 yards] of wire out, obviously the speed of the ship is down to about eight, nine knots. And from out of nowhere it came, the two bangs, great spouts of water. I wasn't so much frightened as amazed.

Did you ever think that we might lose the war?

Oh, I didn't think like that. If you took the view that we might not win the war, that could easily have happened. When you're on the lower deck you don't know what the staff people are talking about. It's only when you get higher up the ladder you know what's going on. We ordinary sailors did what we were told to do, whether it was right or wrong we had no idea. Found out later. The Captain was fantastic – I can think of two examples.

The big difference between the Russian convoys and Malta, where we went later, was visibility. On the way to Russia it was incredibly cold and the visibility was poor, but Malta was just the opposite – you had visibility of twenty miles, more, and cloudless skies. No way of hiding from anything at all. And this feller was on the compass platform on a chair which was turned back, and when the dive bombers came down he actually waited for the bomb to leave the aircraft and then ordered a change of course. Now you've got to have real nerve to do that, knowing that if you're wrong you get it straight down the funnel.

Later on we towed the *Ohio* in, in the August 1942 convoy,

the big one, Pedestal. We went out from Malta to help the escorts. She was 9,514 gross tons, almost awash, no steering or anything like that, and we towed her in. Now that was a feat of seamanship, believe me.

We'd got two ships in in the June convoy – Force H, with the carrier force, had come with us for two days before turning back. We'd taken that convoy from the UK to Gib, and thought we were going back. But in fact we refuelled from the tanker *Kentucky*, sister ship to the *Ohio*, and we all went together to Malta. We left in the dark, so as to camouflage from the Germans and Spaniards who were ashore what was going on – they didn't know if we were going this way or that way. In fact we had gone with Force H.

After she was bombed we had to board the *Kentucky* and put a scuttling charge down below. She was on fire and you could see her for miles, great pall of smoke. Blew the bottom out. She sank, but the fire still burnt as long as we could see it – thousands of tons of oil.

Another Y Scheme entrant was *Hugh Spensley*, who, far from being disillusioned by the reality of life in the Navy – as many were – came to regret not having made different choices when he was younger.

You weren't tempted by the RAF or the Army?
In no way, actually. Totally by the Navy. And I must say, looking back, while I've had an enjoyable and I hope successful career, if I had my time over again I'd have gone into the RN as a regular. I've got such regard for the service.
Had you been to sea before you joined?
Just across the Channel to France!
And did you know any people in the Navy?
I knew a Surgeon Captain, who I went to see because my original idea was that I wanted to be a doctor in the Navy. He rather warned me off this; because he said it was one thing being a doctor, but he didn't think it would suit me becoming a sick bay tiffy [Sick Berth Attendant, a rating]. He said 'I think you should go for a commission, and you obviously can't get a medical commission so you've got to go into the Y Scheme, and get an executive commission.'

I took his advice and was accepted. I was interviewed up in London by I think it was three Captains, RN.

Can you remember what kinds of things they said?

That's something that's difficult to answer – in those days it wasn't as technical as it is now, and I think they were probably more concerned with personality and whether they thought you were officer material. I suppose I must have been in there for about three-quarters of an hour, something like that. But you must appreciate that this merely meant you were a *candidate*. I still had to join as an Ordinary Seaman, and the selection to go forward to *King Alfred* was looked at in much greater detail – I had interviews with the Captain of the battleship I was in, and so on; it was much more on the basis of your record and how you were found to be as a seaman, than on that initial approach. You could be discarded, and never get to *King Alfred* at all.

Presumably a period of time elapsed between the interview and joining?

Only a matter of just a few weeks. And then I joined, went to HMS *Collingwood* at Fareham and did three months' seaman's training – good training; it was a mixture of learning discipline, getting physically fit and gaining self-confidence, as well as the technical side of seamanship and gunnery and so on.

After I'd been at *Collingwood* for a week I went out on leave for the first time and I went into Portsmouth, as a very young, very green Ordinary Seaman, and got caught in a terrific downpour. I went into the local YMCA to dry off, and the lady in there helped me to dry my clothes and asked me to have some tea. She said to have what I wanted – it was all free, because there was a special do on for Dutch seamen that day and they'd all gone to a film show, so to help myself, which I did. She asked all about the service and I was very careful, very security conscious, and didn't say too much – not that I knew anything at that stage! Then she said 'I'd like you to meet my husband afterwards'. Up to this point I don't think I'd seen anything higher than about a Lieutenant-Commander. When the said husband emerged it was Admiral Sir William James, the C.-in-C.! He said 'I'm going past *Collingwood* – I'll run you back.' So this car with the Admiral's flag on drove to *Collingwood* and stopped off opposite the front gate, and out crawled an Ordinary Seaman. By which time the guard on the gate had come to the present arms, and the Master-at-Arms had come running out of the guardhouse, and everyone was panicking like this, and Sir William James said to me, now you face the music! The guard almost dropped his rifle and the Master-at-Arms looked at me as if I was something the cat had brought in, and Admiral James went off absolutely chuckling. That was the sort of person he was – he was an awfully nice man.

Was discipline strict?

Yes, I think it had to be strict initially in that sort of establishment, because they were teaching discipline to a lot of people for the first time. Lack of punctuality was punished. Scruffiness. Drunkenness coming back from on shore. Any form of insubordination.

Did they have any problems enforcing this discipline with the HOs?

My memory of it is that pretty well all of them accepted it, but you got one or two that were the awkward squad that you get wherever. They hadn't volunteered, and they were openly resentful of being in.

After *Collingwood* we went to barracks at Portsmouth, just until we were assigned to our respective ships. My ship, the new battleship HMS *Howe*, was on her first commission; she'd just gone from the builders to Rosyth – in fact the builders had still not quite finished everything – when I joined her. Shortly after that we went up to Scapa Flow, and the idea was that the first three months we'd be doing working-up trials, going through all the various routines like the use of all the guns, and also all the other things that you had to do in terms of seamanship, like towing other ships, and collision mats – great big mats that are hung over the side if you have a hole. You just had to go through everything to learn the ropes. So that was about three months intensive work at Scapa, then we joined the Home Fleet.

We stayed at Scapa for most of the time – we were there just to stop the *Tirpitz*. There was one occasion when the *Tirpitz* came out and we went haring up into the Arctic Circle, but she fortunately went back. I say fortunately because she was the sister ship to the *Bismarck*, and what the *Bismarck* had done to the *Hood* was not something we wanted to happen to us. While of course we were going to be two or even three to one, and could divide her fire, she could have taken one of us before she went.

When you were in the Howe, *did you feel the ship had any particular strengths or weaknesses?*

I could hardly as an Ordinary Seaman say that, but we had total confidence in her. All right the Germans had these two super ships, but there's no evidence on the whole that our ships were worse than theirs. The *Hood* was an old ship, and she was a battle cruiser, not a battleship – she was built for speed rather than with heavy armour, and there was an unlucky hit which went down into the magazine and blew her up.

I think one thing that struck me as being very antiquated, though, on the *Howe* was the old Walrus amphibian. We carried two of them, and they really were rather a laughing stock, because when they were launched from our catapult deck they got up to about ninety miles per hour at the point where they were catapulted off, and then they *slowed down* when they were flying. You always wondered if they were going to just manage to keep clear of the water!

I was in a mess which had fifty-five of us in there, all sleeping in hammocks, which are very comfortable things to sleep in except when the ship is rolling heavily – at one end of the roll you bump into the person on that side of you, and at the other end of the roll you bump into the person on the other side. They were slung just a little too close; but then they had to pack about 1,500 of us into the ship.

Were all 1,500 needed, or were they overmanned?

They were overmanned at all times except action stations, and then you needed everyone. Your cooks and your stewards and all the people that were normally doing what might be called luxury jobs all had an important action station – helping the sick bay staff, or whatever. There was a job for everyone. And it's when you're at action stations that you're doing what you're there for.

I had about seven months in the *Howe*, then I was interviewed for going on to *King Alfred*. There were more interviews when I got down there, at the beginning of the course, which was about three months altogether. We had to learn a lot of things which to an Ordinary Seaman weren't relevant. More gunnery, but gunnery control rather than the actual practical firing of the gun. Navigation, signalling – that was a thing I was a duffer at. I was hopeless at morse and semaphore, and if you didn't get up to a certain standard you had to do more practice during the lunch hours, so I missed my lunch almost every day.

In true service fashion, the would-be officers were left in the dark as to whether they had passed or failed the course until the actual passing out parade.

We were all paraded without being told whether we had passed or not, and that our names would be called out in alphabetical order. If your name was called out that meant you had failed, in which case you were to take one step forward, salute and double off the parade ground. Being an S in the alphabet I had to wait rather a long time to find out, and then I realized they were calling out the Ts, and I was still there!

They wanted, I think, to draw a distinction between those who'd become officers and those who were their friends who were still seamen, to draw a strict dividing line. So there was no time for goodbyes or anything, they had gone back to barracks, been drafted to ships, and they would remain Ordinary Seamen. In a few cases they may have had a second chance, but I think not that many.

They asked us before we left *King Alfred* what was our choice of ship to go to. I was very keen on getting into coastal forces, so I gave as my choice the rather restricted one of: first, MTBs; second, MGBs; third, MTBs. I thought that way I would make the point that I really wanted to get into coastal forces. So they sent me to a cruiser.

Despite the disappointment, he still recalls with affection this first ship in which he served as an officer.

She was a marvellous ship, the *Orion*. I was in her for the Italian landings, Salerno and so on. My action station was the control of the after oerlikons, which were the close range anti-aircraft guns. It was quite an unpleasant action station because it meant I was just in front of 'X' turret, the upper after-facing turret, and when we went in to bombard the coast – and we were bombarding most of the time – her guns would swing round and I could see down the first bit of the rifling of these 6 inch guns. When they fired it was absolutely blistering!

It hasn't left any long-term effects?

Well, I have slight deafness in one ear now, and it could be it was triggered by that, but I don't know.

And you would be in charge of a group manning these oerlikons?

Yes, but as a Midshipman it was fairly nominal. I did have one exciting experience on the ship actually – when we were on our way to Salerno we were attacked by a group of Ju.88s, and the officer of the watch was injured. The Captain called me up to the bridge – I'd just at that point become a Sub-Lieutenant – and told me to take over. All right, he was still around, but to be officer of the watch in a cruiser when I was only nineteen and a half on the way to an amphibious landing, was quite a thrill.

What did it involve?

Much the same as in any situation – keeping station within the squadron and the normal duties of the watchkeeper, giving changes of course and speed and so on. We were one of three cruisers in our squadron, and Admiral Vian was the rather tough Admiral in the *Mauritius*. There's a marvellous story; on one occasion he hoisted the flag signal for eighteen knots, and the *Uganda*, which was the other cruiser besides ourselves, were in a hurry to get the answering signal up – to beat us. On this occasion *Uganda* shackled on the two flags the wrong way round, and whisked up eighty-one knots instead of eighteen! Before they could pull it down Vian had spotted it, and the signal went out 'Congratulations on your phenomenal speed – circle the squadron three times, and take off!' We loved it in *Orion*, but we could just imagine the feeling on the bridge of the *Uganda*.

Did people become superstitious?

[Pause.] At sea, not just in the Royal Navy, it applies just as much to the Merchant Navy, there are superstitions; but I don't think there was the kind of morbid superstition that there was in, say, Bomber Command. Ours were more the long-term superstitions, like being unlucky to sail on a Sunday. That goes right back into the mists of time.

When a ship like the Prince of Wales *was sunk, did a shock wave pass through your ship?*

I think a shock wave went through us, yes, but it was probably a fairly dispassionate one because it happened on the other side of the world. If you *saw* a ship go down that was horrible, and it brought it right home, whatever the ship. If you were with a convoy and you saw a small tramp steamer or whatever go down, a ship is a living thing and that ship was being killed. That to a seaman is dreadful. But if a ship goes down on the other side of the world, even if it's a battleship, I don't think it has the same impact.

If an officer made a blunder, what kind of penalty would he pay?

I think that would depend on the scale of the blunder and whether it was through carelessness or something that couldn't reasonably have been avoided. In wartime there was far greater leeway on this than there would be now. For example, now if you had a collision or a grounding or something like that, it could be the end of your career. In wartime there was so much going on, so many mistakes being made – because after all, we were only trained very briefly in comparison with the RN people – and there were so many ships. I remember on one occasion we were routed along a swept channel, which wasn't very wide, at the same time as another convoy in the opposite direction – and it turned out to be foggy as well! Well, within a matter of an hour we collided with three ships. Now all right, somebody up the line who routed those two convoys down the same swept channel may have got something like the high jump, but as far as we were concerned it was all in a day's work. It was happening all the time. In a war everyone is expendable and the equipment is too.

Not everyone was so keen on becoming part of the Navy machine. *Ben Land* had come from a professional civilian job, so soon came under pressure to train to be an officer. It was pressure he was determined to resist, though life on the lower deck held few attractions for him. He does not share Hugh Spensley's warm memories of the Navy.

I was a wireless operator throughout the war, and I was drafted to the *Curacoa*, a First World War cruiser on which the conditions were absolutely terrible. We were on Atlantic convoys, covering the *Queen Mary* one way and the *Queen Elizabeth* the other. We could never keep up with them. This particular afternoon, in October, we picked up the *Queen Mary*, which used to do an antisubmarine zig-zag. So much on one leg and so much on the other, and so did we. What happened I don't know, but somebody zigged when they should have zagged, and the *Queen Mary* went straight through the middle of the *Curacoa*. There were twenty-six survivors out of four hundred and seventy-odd men. The after part sank immediately, and the fore part – you've got watertight doors all the way through – floated for probably a quarter of an hour. I was right down below and I don't know how I ever got out. Most of the chaps died from oil, their head goes down and it goes up their nose and throat, and that's the end of them. We had to wait until a Polish destroyer came along to pick up survivors.

Before the *Curacoa* got the hammer we had been completely refitted with no end of new equipment for the Russian run, which nobody was looking forward to very much, in fact. So all that equipment was never used, and went to the bottom of the Atlantic.

I lost everything, all I'd got, like a wristwatch which was given to me by my parents, a fountain pen, and all sorts of personal things. You got nothing, just basic issue of white ducks, blue uniform, one blanket, and the rest of it you had to buy. In fact it cost me money for the privilege of belonging to the Navy in the war.

The food was often so bad I didn't eat, I used to go ashore and get myself a decent meal. My father was furious, so he decided to lobby his MP. Well, the MP for Epping at that stage was a certain Mr Churchill. My father persevered, and in the end Churchill's secretary wrote and said although Mr Churchill was a busy man as my father appreciated, he would see him. But my mother meanwhile was getting rather worried that it would come back on me, so she persuaded him not to go ahead. I was angry when I got back, because this was what we wanted – we were writing to newspapers about the shocking conditions at Chatham barracks, none of which would print anything.

I was never in Chatham barracks for long, thank God. Conditions weren't very far removed from Nelson's day. The barracks was the worst Victorian building that you could ever imagine. The parade ground was vast and it had a big arch which said 'Fear God and honour the King'. It was reputed that you had to hold your plate down otherwise the cockroaches would lift it and run away with it – I've never seen cockroaches like it. At one stage they had an outbreak of TB there and the doctors found it was years of incessant swabbing and cleaning the floor – in between the floorboards you got the bacilli.

Ratings weren't allowed to walk on the pavement, officers only – privileges! Ratings had to double across the parade ground, every time. Now if you're on draft you've got a hammock on your shoulder, a kitbag, a case, a hatbox, and you can imagine trying to double across with this lot! One thing I'll say about the Navy, they made no provision or effort at all to recognize that the chaps coming in were intelligent. I served with bank managers, chaps who had damn good jobs in civvy street, and a lot of them had no desire to advance in rank. They wanted to fight Hitler, get the war over with, and get back to work again. But the Navy made no adjustments to meet an inflow of chaps who were not the same types they'd been having.

After a while they were pushing me, pushing me to take a commission. The Skipper said 'Look, why haven't you gone in for a commission?' I said I don't want a commission, all I want to do is a good job and get out of it. He said 'Well I can't understand you'. I said, quite frankly, I don't want to be in the Navy after the war, and if I get a commission I'll be in the RNVR and after the war they can call me up every two years for training, and I don't need this.

He goes and recommends me for a commission.

I was taken off there and went to *King Alfred*, the officer training place. I went in and this officer with gold braid has got model ships. He said 'If this ship's coming this way and she's showing a red light, and this ship's coming the other way and she's showing a green light, this one turns and does this, what steps would you take?' I said, 'bloody great long ones!'

Do you know, they shoved me under arrest. I think I got ten days leave stopped and was drafted almost immediately.

7

SOLDIERS AT SEA

The Second World War brought another major break with tradition, when the British Army was called upon to assist with the manning of merchant ships.

The Navy's own DEMS (Defensively Equipped Merchant Ship) organization, which provided merchant ships with guns and gunners as well as training merchant seamen in basic gunnery, was swamped by the massive demands of the war, and in February 1940 the Admiralty was driven to ask the Army for help. Five hundred infantrymen were formed into two-man Lewis and Bren teams and embarked in coasters to give them some anti-aircraft defence. Subsequently, in September 1940, the scheme was expanded to place 2,000 men on coasters at sea and a further 2,000 on ships in port.

Stan Philps was called up into the Army for service with the Welch Regiment, but was surprised to find himself detailed almost immediately for merchant ship protection.

I'm not sure how many of us they sent; there was quite a lot, about nine platoons, and we were all sent off onto this job. Now this was just after Dunkirk, so I suppose the figuring of the top brass was that it didn't matter if the uniform was blue or khaki so long as the wearer could shoot a small arm, that was the main point. So they started forming two-man teams, each man with a machine gun. Of course that's a thousand yards limited range, but at least we had incendiary bullets, and tracer and armour piercing, as well as the ordinary .303, so if we did get a hit it went through – especially if it was armour piercing. The fall of France had opened the shores of England to direct air attack – the Germans could send their bombers across, and the merchant ships were sitting ducks. So they decided to put some machine-gunners on, anything being better than nothing, and they put us onto the boats because the Navy at the time couldn't supply the necessary. We went on there as a temporary thing. They didn't even bother to give us a regiment, because I presume they believed we were going to be hauled off the job as fast as the Navy could train personnel to take over from us. Then they would be just simply DEMS, and no Army at all.

But in fact the Army's role aboard merchant ships became a permanent one, lasting right to the end of the war. In February 1941 it was decided to expand the scheme to include all merchant ships, deep sea as well as coastal, and in May the organization was put on a formal footing. Its gun teams were transferred from their original infantry units to the Royal Artillery, and formed into the 1st, 2nd, 3rd and 4th Maritime Anti-Aircraft Regiments, RA.

Some of us were sent to Falmouth, a favourite port to meet ships coming in from America and Canada. I and my mate, both Lance Corporals, were put aboard an Estonian boat. They couldn't speak any English, so there was no conversation between us at all. We started our maritime AA duties aboard that ship, and I nearly ended mine.

We went all along the south coast, through the Channel, until we were somewhere opposite the Wash. Everything seemed as safe as houses, with the weather sunny and warm. While my mate sat by the Lewis, which was supported by a metal rod sunk into a big lump of concrete, I took a turn around the deck in my shirt sleeves.

I did hear a plane and should have reacted to it immediately, but by the time I'd begun running along the deck to get to my own gun, this German plane had started machine gunning the bridge from for'ard, and then turned his attention to us. My mate was quick off the mark and opened up on him, hitting him, but nothing serious. The German gunner turned his belt-fed gun on me, but the bullets were landing about ten feet behind me, as I ran. Of course, the poor chap had great difficulty in getting the correct aim off. Well, you don't expect a running man to be breaking the four minute mile, do you?

Noone on the ship was hurt. Everyone had scarpered down below when the attack began, including the helmsman, so the boat rolled and rocked. There were about a dozen women on board, who were cooks, helpers, maids, and so on, and when they all came on deck they went around gathering up the bent and buckled German bullets as souvenirs.

When the Navy started putting on bigger guns, oerlikons, twelve pounders, 4 inch, I suppose the Army said to them what about our fellers, why should you have all Navy gunlayers – why can't you have Army gunlayers? So they said all right, every twenty-eight man class, seven of them can be Army chaps. I always remember the Commander on this gunlayers' course, he was only a little man, he would say 'Leading Seaman so-and-so'. As you all stood there at ease, the individual whose name is called jumps to attention so he can see the movement and see who it is. He'd glower at this man and there'd be a long pause, and he'd say 'Failed!' Failed – as if it was something to commit suicide over. And somebody else – he'd perk up 'passed'. When it came to us Army he'd say 'passed' without any enthusiasm!

We were supposed to be able to serve in all the positions round the gun – breech operator, or trainer – that's the bloke that swings the gun from left to right – or gunlayer – he would swing it up and down. Gunlayer was the most difficult job, because the guns were always perched on the end of the ship, and of course the tail end of a ship goes up and down like this in the water, so all the time you're having to keep the muzzle up and down against the motion. The best thing I found was to wait till you're right rock bottom or right up high, when the ship's come up to the point where it's about to go down again, fire then, because just for a few seconds you've got a steady platform.

It was one thing for the gunners manning the ships to be trained by the Royal Navy or the Army or whatever, but they were supposed to be civilian gunners! So every ship we went on, the Captain was given papers claiming we were deckhand gunners. I mean we weren't, but that was in case we went – as we often did – to neutral countries. In a neutral country you couldn't go ashore in uniform – the Army provided us with a pair of flannels and an old sports jacket each – and as soon as you got within about three miles of the place, you'd slip the breech blocks out of any big guns you'd got, and put 'em in like a locker room with all the ammunition and stuff.

DEMS gun crews mixed Army, Merchant Navy, Royal Navy and Marines up together. What differences did you find between them?

We got a lot less pay than the merchant seamen got with their danger money! The merchant seamen used to moan and say we're stuck out here doing this job, we've got friends who've got jobs in factories and they're earning any amount of money, we're risking our lives out here. And I'd say to them, don't forget me, mate! I've never been to sea in my life before, I've never been on a boat – the Army just detailed me. You, you and you. We were running the risk and they were getting the money!

The Marines, they had a book of instructions about quarter of an inch or three-eighths of an inch thick, and they would go like that and chuck you the book and say open it anywhere you like, give me the top of the page. And away they'd go. They knew the flipping book backwards! Absolutely parrot fashion. Everything according to them should be done parrot fashion.

Anyway, we went off to sea again, and we were gone about a year – that was the time we got torpedoed and couldn't get on another ship to get back home again.

We had a warning at about six o'clock in the morning – the buzz went round that a ship somewhere about twenty-five miles ahead of us on an identical course had been torpedoed. The Captain said, if we stick the way we are, then allowing for the time lag, the U-boat could be anyplace. The only thing is, we'll stay on our course and just hope for the best. Hope that having nobbled a ship at that spot at that latitude and longitude, he'll go somewhere else. If we go to the left, that might be where he's gone; and if we go to the right that might be where he's gone.

So they set ten or eleven lookouts, keeping a sharp eye out. But all you can see is just a little periscope, and if the U-boat slows right down there won't be any wake from it. Seeing the thing itself is pretty difficult to say the least, and what can you do about it even if you do see it? If he got the opportunity the

Skipper could turn the ship to the U-boat and hope that the width is too narrow to be hit, but that's about it.

Just after eight bells my mate Brownie and me came off watch, and the Second Engineer and the mess boy were sitting there – mess boy! Man of thirty-two married with two children! – and I remember the engineer asking me if I'd read the news. See, the crew had no radios, so the wireless operator used to listen to the news and he used to jot down things like two hundred bombers raided Dresden, or whatever, he used to jot down the actual details – numbers and places – then when the news broadcast was finished he used to write it all out in longhand. So you didn't say to somebody 'Have you heard the news?', you said 'Have you read the news?'. Normally I'd have stopped, but my breakfast was getting cold, so I said I'll get that later, and strolled past, up the companionway to the gunners' cabin. Took off my life-jacket and stuck it down. I'd had about three mouthfuls of porridge, while Brownie went to the toilet, and when he came back he was just in time to hear the bang. The whole ship heaved up, over the table I went, grabbed my life-jacket – I can't swim, or couldn't then – so I'm putting my life-jacket on, and Brownie goes down to the deck.

Now a torpedo travels at a terrific speed, and as it does so it drags a great big wave behind it, which also hits the ship. We were loaded and down low in the water, so this wave carried right across the deck, so by the time I'd gone outside, Brownie's half way or three-quarters of the way across the lower level deck, and this tidal wave picks him up and carries him right over the guard rail and out into the sea beyond. You see it happen and you think it can't happen, but it just did.

The liferafts were on runners, and there was a little hammer hanging there, so I picked up the hammer and banged the interlinked catch, and this raft hits the water and ends up about twenty feet away from the side of the ship. Brownie's out there swimming away like mad to get to it. He's all right, so I suppose I should go on the gun platform, that's what we're told to do. I go up there and the other blokes are there, the other three, making four of us out of the five gunners. So the gunlayer said 'Where's Brownie?'. I said he got swept over the bloody side!

We're all lying flat on the deck so that hopefully the U-boat if he's looking through his periscope can't see us. The idea is that we're going to do what the Admiralty and the War Office say – close up to the gun and load it and fire at the U-boat that sinks you, while the ship's still steady. Because the Germans didn't want to waste torpedoes – torpedoes that have to be brought all the way from Germany – so therefore it might take twenty minutes for the ship to sink.

But along came the Mate with about half a dozen seamen, after this small boat on the gun deck. 'What are you doing up here?' he said. So the gunlayer said 'Our Army and Navy instructions are we're supposed to stand by the gun, and when the U-boat comes up, we're to shoot at it'. 'You're going to shoot at nothing! What do you want – us all bloody murdered? The ship's gone', he said, 'there's nothing we can do about it. Get the hell out of it – there's room in the lifeboat amidships.' So I said to the gunlayer, 'Well that's it mate, I'm in charge of the Army here and you're in charge of the Navy, but both of us have to obey the ship's officers, so to hell with the Admiralty and the War Office, two fingers to 'em – we're off!' We didn't want to be heroes anyway, I can assure you, we wanted to get out.

The Captain was the last one off. We checked up and found the two people missing were the Second Engineer and the mess boy. They must have been right where the torpedo exploded. And the poor old donkeyman, he's the chappie who goes around with the oil can greasing things, when the torpedo struck it must have struck at least one of the boilers because this poor feller, he's just wearing slippers and a pair of trousers and a sweatband round his neck – we were in the tropics – and when the boiler went off he must for want of a better description have been cooked alive, because all the steam went straight up through him, so his skin was just hanging off him in strips. We had a Second Mate who was a right so-and-so, silly bugger, he used to go to sleep on watch and all sorts of weird and wonderful things, but when it came to it he was right on the ball, when other people were panicking he kept calm, giving instructions and so on, apparently he heard this poor fellow screaming, and though he didn't have to he went back and down into the boiler room and got this poor chap over his shoulders and hauled him up and into the lifeboat. They got him under an awning they'd put up in the bows to keep him away from the sun. Of course the sun – oh God, what the poor fellow would have experienced with the sun shining on him, and all these strips of flesh . . . [shudders].

The crew spent three days and two nights in the lifeboats before making landfall on the island of Tobago. They were then taken by ship to New Orleans, where the artillerymen were put on a train to New York.

When we got to New York we joined a draft of seventy of us. Now on average we only had four or five men on every ship, so that gives you some idea of how many ships were sunk, for that number of chaps. So they said to us 'We've made arrangements with the US Marines for you to be put up in their barracks', to meet the need. They came down with lorries to meet the train, and a Top Sergeant was allocated to us to sort out any problems. America was in the war by that time so we could go about in uniform, and they even paid us while we were there.

The only problem was that our blokes, during the day, had nothing to do. One day the Top Sergeant came to us and said how about if we took over one of the gates for twenty-four hours – actually stood guard over the American Marine barracks. We said yes – it was something to tell people when we got home!

There were three gates, and not having been in the war long they were very lackadaisical about security. They used to let their marines go out and come back with or without a pass – if they left the barracks to go down the road to the coffee shop or something they'd just come wandering back in, casual like. So we do this guard and we post our sentries, and along come a couple of marines to wander down the road and get a cup of cawffee [laughs]. 'Pass!' 'Huh?' 'Pass! Got to see your pass! You know, that little bit of paper that says you're allowed to leave the barracks.' 'We ain't got no passes.' 'Then you don't leave the barracks.' Go to the sentry box, take out the clipboard, say 'Here – read those instructions for sentries! And who's signed it? Your commanding officer. This is what you fellows are supposed to be doing. They aren't doing it but this is what they're supposed to be doing. We're the British and we *are* doing it. If you want to go out, mate, you'll have to go down one of the other gates.' They couldn't believe it. Couldn't leave their own barracks. Some of them come up the road, prepare to come in. 'Pass!' 'Uh?' 'We want your pass!' Out with the clipboard again, 'What does it say here?' 'But you can see we're marines, we're wearing the uniform.' 'Yes, you are mate, but a few hundred yards down there is the surplus stores. You can buy umpteen thousand of the things down there – you could be anybody!' When this got back to the American officers, they thought it was hilarious, really good.

Anyway, from there they said the likelihood of getting a ship was remote, but up in Canada they were building a lot of ships and sending them off, so once more on the train, all the way up to St John in New Brunswick. We were billeted in the Merchant Navy Club, and drafts of about a dozen or so went off to different places, so we were more or less split up.

As the Army's maritime commitment expanded, small pools of replacement personnel were established in the major British-controlled ports around the world. In command of each was usually an NCO, whose job was to run his own small detachment and to carry out inspections of visiting ships to make sure the gun teams felt less isolated. It was to just such a job that Stan was posted in mid-1943.

This place where I was, Vizagapatam, was the fifth largest port in India during peacetime. I expect it was in wartime as well, because they had a lot of ships in and out of there – from the Persian Gulf, or round the tip of Africa. I used to go on board the ships and inspect the guns and see if they'd got any problems, that the ammunition was up to date, and oh, a hundred and one different jobs. And the funny part was, it all came under me – an Army Sergeant. It was a very mixed outfit.

As most ships I went out to inspect at the buoys hadn't yet lowered a companionway, I nearly always had to do a steeple-jack climb up a vertical Jacob's ladder. My flaming Army gaiters always caught their tops on the underneath of the next rung up, so it became an awkward thing to do, holding my leg back each step, to clear the gaiters from the rungs!

Relations between khaki and blue were not always smooth, partly because of the Army gunners' anomalous position – paid by the Army but quartered by the Navy – and partly because of their detachments having only NCOs to speak for them. When disputes arose, considerable guile was often required to resolve them in the Army's favour.

I said to this Captain at the naval base, HMIS *Circars*, that I couldn't comply with his request. He assured me it wasn't a request, it was a bloody order. I said I couldn't accept that, and would have to see what my big boss had to say about it. He said I could see who the hell I liked, my unit was in his barracks, and I might as well get used to the idea he was taking over my transport.

The big boss I had in mind – though I didn't know then whether it would work – was no less a personage than the Brigadier, Royal Artillery who resided in the fort overlooking Vizag. At the time the Brig. didn't know we existed – he controlled coast defence, but we came under the War Office back in the UK. However, it was very doubtful if the Captain, RN would know that, and to him a Brig. is a Brig.

After the meeting the Captain, RN, had had his nose put out of joint, but I mollified him by telling the Brig. that the Captain had been kind enough to grant us the fine accommodation we had, and would he thank the Captain for that, so the Captain was pleased to be thanked.

I figured he could say afterwards for spite – to get his own back – that he needed our accommodation for someone else, after all he was the boss of *Circars*. But he could hardly do so after the Brig. had thanked him for it!

8

FLEET AIR ARM

When the Royal Air Force was formed as a separate service in April 1918, the Navy's aircraft (flown by what was then known as the Royal Naval Air Service) were arbitrarily transferred to it. A compromise agreement whereby a Fleet Air Arm of the RAF existed under dual control between 1924 and 1939 did little to redress the Navy's sense of grievance over this, and in May 1939 the Air Ministry finally handed back the entire Fleet Air Arm, complete with shore bases.

Although the Royal Navy had the largest carrier fleet in the world when war broke out, only one of its seven ships – the 22,000 ton *Ark Royal* – was less than twenty years old. The aircraft too were either obsolete or obsolescent, with offensive capability being provided by the Fairey Swordfish and fighter cover by the Blackburn Skua or Gloster Sea Gladiator, which hardly compared favourably with the RAF's new Hurricanes and Spitfires.

Near the start of 1939 every household in the country was sent a booklet detailing the various options for National Service. *Cyril Corpes* was one eager reader, then just short of his seventeenth birthday.

The booklet had all the suggestions for joining like the Territorial Army and the equivalents but one of the things that caught my eye was for a year's full-time training on the pilot/observer's air flying course.

As a youth I was interested in flying, and of course my father and his father before him were regulars in the Navy. My father was killed in 1940. He served in the First World War, twenty-two years from 1909 to 1931 – Heligoland Bight, Dogger Bank, Battle of Jutland, all the big battles in the war – and came out without a scratch. But as a pensioner and reservist, although he was nearly fifty, he was still recalled. He went to sea and was lost with his ship in 1940.

Being modern-minded I was interested in flying, and in the Navy, so I tried to combine the two. I signed on for aircrew. When I applied I said I would prefer pilot but would accept observer, and in the event I became an observer. It made no difference as regards rank and all the rest of it. In the Navy practically all pilots and observers were commissioned.

We had to do our training as naval ratings at that time. If you didn't pass your exams you didn't get your commission. You were either allowed to drop out or transfer to something else. Some became air gunners.

I had the medical exam in June 1939, and at the end of July-August they said I'd been accepted and would start my training in October. In the meantime the war had started anyway, and of course once I was in I was in. Although I'd signed on before, by the time I was commissioned the war was well and truly on and they only gave us temporary commissions.

We had to go in with secondary school education, which obviously included maths, and the basis of navigation is the old triangle of forces. If your aircraft is flying in *that* direction and the wind is blowing in *that* direction, then of course your track over the ground is *that* direction. That's it basically, though you've got all sorts of things to take into account. If you're flying from a moving ship you've got to record the direction and speed of the ship, as you've got to come out and get back to it.

Can you remember your first flight?

Yes, it was in a Percival Proctor – a civil aircraft. We didn't have any fitments at all. We didn't even carry radar, and we weren't allowed to fly over the sea in it. That was in our very initial flying training. They used to take up two trainee observers at a time – one would have a go and do something, and then the other. My very first trip there were two trainees plus the pilot and it was very, very bumpy weather. All three of us including the trained pilot were sick [*laughs*]. I started off, a lot of us did, being sick at first. It's something akin to seasickness I suppose. But I got accustomed to it, and when I got to sea I was never seasick!

After successfully completing his training at Ford and Arbroath flying the Blackburn Shark and Supermarine Walrus, he was posted to a squadron equipped with the Fairey Albacore, which the Navy intended should replace the Swordfish. The squadron had only just been formed, and was earmarked for the new carrier HMS *Formidable*, then fitting out at the Harland & Wolff yard in Belfast.

We joined the carrier in Belfast; it was a brand new one. After we'd done two or three weeks ship's acceptance trials between Belfast and Greenock, then perhaps back into Belfast for a few days for modifications and so on, we went up to Scapa.

What were conditions like on board? Pretty crowded?

Well, I was the most junior officer on board, and because I was under twenty I was only made a Midshipman to begin with. There were about five of us Midshipmen, and we had an Admiral on board. That overloads the accommodation you might say, because of him and his staff. There were not enough cabins to go round for all the officers, so we junior ones had to sling hammocks in the gangways outside the other officers' cabins. When it got too hot for that we had folding camp beds on the deck. I never had a cabin. I used to share one with another officer for washing – had to go in and wash and shave and so on.

What about the discipline?

Discipline on the ship was what you might call normal ship's discipline, especially on a large ship. You find on small things like destroyers and that discipline was usually a bit more lax. On the carrier it was a bit more pukka. But we didn't used to have inessential discipline, just somebody shouting their heads off for the sake of it. I got on very well with all the senior officers. Our own squadron CO was very strict but he was very fair; he'd give you a rip-roaring telling off for something to do with your flying, but back in the mess it'd be 'Have a drink' sort of thing.

Were you separate from the ship's company?

No, no. We all mixed up. Same mess. We had three squadrons, each squadron had its own Lieutenant-Commander. Then above them was the Commander (Flying), who was a pilot – he didn't fly as aircrew, but he had done in the past – in charge of flying operations. He was up on the bridge for the launching of aircraft and things like that. And there was also a Commander (Air Staff) who was an observer. He used to be in command of the operational side, working out things and giving all the gen, necessary – the information the aircraft were likely to need on patrol. Then there was the Batsman [Deck Landing Control Officer], the chap in charge of landing aircraft on, waving his bats around. One or two odd people like that. The Commander (Flying) came under the Captain of the carrier.

I was flying Albacores all the time I was on operations. We were the first two squadrons, 826 and 829, to go to sea so we were the first two Albacore squadrons to arrive out in Egypt. We'd lost one or two aircraft on the way round from the UK via Cape Town for various reasons, so when we got into Egypt we took temporary replacements of Swordfish. As soon as the Albacore replacements came through the Swordfish were got rid of. I did fly to Cyprus in one, though.

How did the two compare?

The Albacore had dive brakes which the Swordfish didn't, and it had a glasshouse, which was more comfortable for the crew. The rear gun was a 'K', which was gas-operated, rather than the Lewis – the Swordfish had the old Lewis – the 'K' had a faster rate of fire. Official bombload was the same, though we used to fly overloaded sometimes.

I wasn't a pilot, I was an observer, but the pilots used to say the Swordfish would fly itself, it was so easy. It was certainly highly manoeuvrable. It was slow of course, but the Albacore was only five knots faster.

We were completely separate from the pilot. In the Swordfish the pilot was above the main planes, then there was a bulkhead and then you and the air gunner, the three in line. In the Albacore the pilot was for'ard of the main plane, a lovely view – a much better view on the Albacore, though his view astern wasn't so good. Sometimes we used to fly with a long range tank in. That was stuck in behind the main tank; the observer sat in the air gunner's position, and the air gunner didn't fly. Just the two of us then. It gave us an extra hour or two.

In May 1941 the *Formidable* was crippled by an air attack, and her aircraft were flown on shore.

I was on the carrier till she was damaged. We went to Alexandria to make her seaworthy, because when we got back to Alex, you could stand on the quay and look right through the ship – her guts were blown out both sides. If we'd gone too fast the waves would have gone in, but they patched up the outside to make her seaworthy and she went off to America for major repairs.

Without a carrier the Navy loaned our whole squadron complete to the RAF's Desert Air Force. Tedder[5] came out and saw us all. We used to get our ops information from them. Our orders were the enemy were in retreat, our forces were advancing. Such-and-such a line was to be the limit, everything to the west of that line is your meat. Our forces were coming this way, so anything east of that line might be our own. Well, the advance was going so quickly – they were not just creeping forward; all the trucks and vehicles were racing on, the enemy were in mad retreat – that in the space of an hour or two our forces had crossed that line. And they were attacked by our own people. But there you are – it happens everywhere. It isn't anybody's fault. It's just lack of information, or in this case the advance was so quick nobody anticipated they would get that far.

How did you get on with the RAF people?

Oh, OK. We shared their mess with them – Blenheim squadrons – and we used to operate with them. It was all very friendly. The Blenheim full load was four 250 pounders. They were a twin engined aircraft and much faster than us, and had a longer range. They looked aghast when they saw us carrying six 250s!

Our mess consisted of a wooden hut with a marquee at one end where they used to cook, and there was another wooden hut operations room, but we were all sleeping under canvas. In

---

[5] Air Marshal Arthur Tedder, C-in-C RAF Middle East

the evening, the coolest part of the day, we used to have a game of rounders or baseball. We were standing out there one evening listening to the Wellingtons starting up ready to go off on their op. – we could acually see them in the distance – just getting dusk, night attack. And there was a Godalmighty bang – we saw the flash before we heard the bang – and one of these had blown up. They apparently had started using delayed action bombs, which scattered across their target and might be several hours before they went off. They reckoned that somebody had accidentally dropped or knocked the fuse, or knocked the bomb, perhaps while it was being loaded onto the aircraft, which might be several hours before take-off – and without knowing it they had actuated the fuse, so that in one case when the aircraft was on the ground, and the other when it was over the sea, the bomb had gone off.

Then we had the rumour that we were going to get some of these bombs! Oh dear! But fortunately we didn't. We had a variety of bombs, tail-fuse or nose-fuse. Because we were attacking surface things – aircraft on aerodromes, motor transport workshops, stores, quaysides and installations – not only did we put an instantaneous nose-fuse on but we used to put a rod about so big [about a yard long] with a flat plate at the end so that not only was it instantaneous, but in effect the bomb exploded above the ground. Instead of just making a big crater and the blast going upwards, the blast went straight out. We must have done a lot of damage with the bomb splinters flying about.

How did you find your targets?

Well, some of the targets were obvious. We used to attack the harbour at Port Bardia quite easily. We usually used to come in over the sea, because if you're flying out over land you would be giving more warning. Once we'd attacked we used to come back over land. With things further inland it was dead reckoning navigation.

As observers we were trained for level bombing with a bomb-sight, but I never actually did it on ops. We always did dive bombing, which is the pilot's pigeon. We used to dive so low that we used to feel the blast from our own bombs.

How many ops constituted a tour?

Oh, we didn't have that in the Navy. One chap in particular was in it for three years solid; he joined as a Midshipman and finished up as CO. After about eighteen months they reckoned you could start asking for a rest. I got one because I was injured, which was just by accident. The squadron was issued with several crates full of captured Italian rifles for ground defence. Though normally we were about a hundred miles behind the front line there was always the possibility of enemy paratroops coming in, so they armed us with these rifles. I was having a bit of target practice when the breech blew back and I got a tiny splinter, only minute, the size of a pinhead, in my left eye. We were just outside Tobruk at the time, went into Tobruk hospital and they tried an electromagnet, and so forth; came back to the UK, had another medical and they grounded me. I said look, I've heard of pilots flying – look at old Bader, with two artificial legs. They said no. I don't know whether they were extra fussy or what, but they wouldn't let me fly again.

Sometimes I think perhaps it was fortunate. I could have been killed. I did fifteen months of ops as it was. I'd known chaps in our squadron, very first flight they'd be killed. Just the luck of the draw.

After I was grounded I was sent as a squadron staff officer to a pilots' training school up in Scotland. I was there for about twenty months, and several of the chaps who'd been in the squadron with me in the desert arrived up there. There was no fixed stint, but they were taken off ops. Not only for their own benefit – to have a bit of a rest – but to pass on their knowledge to the trainees coming through. They used to come to Crail as qualified pilots, they'd got their wings, but they had to do their operational flying training.

The remorseless expansion of the FAA meant a soaring demand for crews, and increasing numbers of trainees came to be sent to Canada or the United States for instruction. *Geoffrey Wright* was one of the British pilots to find himself in America, and an object of considerable curiosity.

Oh, it was a bit embarassing. 'Say, Limey, say somet'n. Say

somet'n. Hey, listen to this, kids! Here's a Limey! Go on, say somet'n . . .' This was Bobbie [shows me photo]. She lived beside Sing Sing prison. And this one I said 'What does your father do?' 'He drives the back end of a fire engine.' It's true! The back ends would steer! These are the photographs sent home to my mother and father; censor's cut that out because it's the radar.

Your parents knew what you were doing?

Yes, more or less. We weren't able to tell them, but they gathered what it was. That's my plane [more photos]; that was Stupid, the monkey we had. He was a lovely little fellow.

You had American instructors all the time you were there?

Yes. Some were very, very nice, like Lieutenant Teebow – he would sing the whole time in what he fondly imagined to be a cockney accent. He sat in the front cockpit, and on the back of his helmet he'd got a huge 'Relax Relax Relax!' At the end of training, he said 'Your father's a clergyman Wright? How many Psalms are there?' '150 sir!' 'Right, I'll write the 151st Psalm.' And he wrote in the log book 'Remember thine airspeed lest the ground rise up and smite thee.' The Commander, the British one, said he was defacing His Majesty's log book! [shows me the book. In it is written 'Remember the 151st Psalm – keep thine airspeed lest the ground rise up and smite thee but hard!!! Rules for living – Control your emotions. Think independently. Act courageously'] He was a lovely man; he went on Avengers and was killed. And yet some of the others were real bastards. Some of the Americans hated the British. They had this very Germanic system that after every little failure you had to have a check by another instructor. If he gave you an upcheck, with an up arrow, you were OK. If you got a downcheck you had to have another test by another instructor. If he gave you a downcheck you were out. Two downchecks and you were finished. After one downcheck you had to get two upchecks, so you had test after test after test. And if you got two in a row who didn't like the British . . .

Was there a pattern to it? If they were Irish?

Could be. Or if they were French Canadian in origin. Or if they were Catholics from Boston. But they were deeply harsh on their own too. They chucked out lots of students. The failure rate was terrific.

The training was very compartmentalized. I didn't particularly like that. You'd go to one field to do formation flying, and you did formation flying, formation flying, until you were sick of it. And then you went and did instruments. You were under that hood flying patterns, and you had to memorize those patterns. You had to fly north climbing at 500 feet a minute for one minute, then do a 270 degree turn to port, descending 500 feet a minute, all on instruments. If we got the pattern wrong they didn't bother us, but if the American cadets forgot it they made them get a hoop and go round the parade ground about twenty times to make them remember. And if you came in with your wheels up – because after a fixed undercarriage plane it was hard to remember the Harvard had to have the wheels put down – then they made the American cadets take an aircraft tyre and a stick and pat it round wherever they went! They could go into Pensacola to the cinema but they still had to take their tyre. You'd see a row of these tyres outside the cinema! And out would come these cadets and pat off with their tyres! Very childish. They were full of bullshit, of course. At Fort Lauderdale they had 'Beneath these portals pass the World's best fliers', so the senior British officer over his office door had put 'Beneath these portals pass the World's worst fliers'!

I was keen on going on fighters, but it was the usual business – they wanted three for torpedo bombers, you, you and you. So I got sent to Fort Lauderdale for training. That was quite a jump because they had no dual control ones. This big 54 foot Avenger – you were just sent from a Harvard straight onto that solo.

Went from Fort Lauderdale up to New York, from New York to Boston; at Boston we worked up a new squadron, 897; came back to Scotland to Machrihanish, did some flying there; went over to Belfast and did some more flying there; then out to Ceylon. From there we went and flew on to the *Indomitable*. That was quite something, because the only carrier flying we'd done was on one in Chesapeake Bay with the Americans, where they gave you some initial deck landing training. I remember I was the last one to land on, and the Commander (Flying) came up and said 'That landing was quite good. What speed were you doing?' I hadn't a clue because I hadn't been looking. So I said 78 knots sir! 'Well, that's the official speed it'll be then!' So how many people stalled because I gave the wrong speed I don't know! It was fairly critical, because you just had to be about 2 knots above the stall. If you had the tail too far down you stalled; if you had the tail too far up your hook didn't catch the arrester wires.

So we joined the *Indomitable*, bombed an enemy oil well then went on to Australia to become part of the British Pacific Fleet. In those days of course we did have a fleet. There was the battleship *King George V*, umpteen cruisers and destroyers, an enormous lot. From there we went up into the Pacific and were bombing Japanese-held airfields in support of the Okinawa landings. They kept threatening that we were going to go and do torpedoes, but luckily we didn't because the torpedo run was really suicide. One whole squadron got lost doing a torpedo attack – you had to fly straight and level at 300 feet, usually at a battleship which was shooting everything at you. But we didn't. We were dive bombing.

How did you form up your crew?

Allocated. You didn't have the slightest choice. I know in the RAF the pilot was the Captain – he could be a Sergeant, and his navigator could be a Squadron Leader, but he was still in charge. Not so with the Navy. There was a crew of three in the Avenger – two officers, the pilot and the observer, and the telegraphist/air gunner, who was always a Petty Officer – and it was the senior one who was in charge. I happened to have been an officer a month longer than my observer, so I was the Captain, but if he'd been a month more than me he'd have been the Captain. I never saw my air gunner away from flying.

Were you a separate group on the carrier? Did you have to stand watches?

This was one of these weird businesses, and one of the things I didn't like about the Navy. They did their best to assimilate you and make you forget that you were a flier, but it wasn't very easy (a) because you weren't trained for anything else and (b) because you were busy anyway. So they got their own back.

They made you do second officer of the watch in harbour, things like that.

What did that involve?

That was a rotten job, because the first officer of the watch stayed on the wardroom deck aft, where the officers came aboard. But we had to do the gangway amidships, protected by a couple of Royal Marines and a Master-at-Arms, to decide whether the ratings coming back were drunk or not [laughs]. He's all right; he's all right; to the cells; he's all right; he's all right; take him to the cells! And you weren't very popular, one took a swipe at the officer! That only meant he got about four times as long a sentence.

Did you have a separate mess?

No, you were either an officer or you weren't. If you were an officer you were in the wardroom, and if you were a Petty Officer you were in the PO's mess, and if you were a Chief Petty Officer you were in the CPO's mess – if you had two air gunners together it didn't matter, you were either a CPO, in the CPO's mess, or a PO in the PO's mess, or a rating in a rating's mess. It was definitely by rank and not by anything else, although I strongly suspect the RN pinched all the decent things! They seemed to – they certainly looked down on the aircrew in that we got the rotten cabins and that sort of thing. In the American Navy the carrier was based round the aircrews, but no, the ship was a Royal Navy ship and you got your desserts according to rank.

Curious, given that the whole purpose of the ship was the flying!

Ah, that didn't matter. That didn't cut any ice whatsoever. Of course the carrier wasn't built for the Far East – it had a 3 inch steel flight deck! It was hot as hell. Everyone had something wrong with them – prickly heat – and it was just very depressing. The refrigerators all broke down, so we had nothing but dry potatoes and sardines on toast. We were three months at sea without ever touching land. We'd come down from the operating area and up would come a hospital ship to take off wounded, and a fuelling tanker to fuel us, and a supply ship to bring us supplies, and then off we'd go again.

I had a friend who was in the *King George V*, and in the Admiralty Islands when we were resting up there I got a signal from the *KGV* – Lieutenant Commander Rule requests the presence of Sub-Lieutenant Wright for tea at 1600 hrs in the wardroom. So I sent back a signal – WMP, with much pleasure. Got out my least scruffy whites. He sent over this Admiral's barge for me, and I was taken across to her. What a difference! As I say, this crowded, smelly, stinking aircraft carrier, against this battleship. He had a cabin the size of this room; white-jacketed stewards bringing you cucumber sandwiches, literally! Oh dear, it was superb.

Were you ever attacked by Japanese aircraft?

Yes, funnily enough I don't think I ever saw one when it was doing the attacking but I jolly well know it was there because I could see the bullets hitting the next plane – going into the wing! I saw these black holes appearing bup-bup-bup! Stitching their way along. I thought oh, it's coming towards me. But then one of our fighters shot him down before he actually got there. I think the plane was hit a few times, but I wasn't. I never suffered a scratch.

I've never been superstitious. I never bothered if there was a thirteen on the plane. I had the photographic plane, 377, and the day I didn't fly it it was flown by a friend of mine and he got shot down in it. But I didn't attach any significance to that except that I lost my plane and I had to pack up my friend's things, which wasn't very pleasant. And read all the letters to see if they were suitable to be sent home or not. That wasn't so good.

What were the losses like?

Well, you see there were so many spheres. I think the earlier part of the war, say on the Murmansk run and things like that, they were far heavier. And in the Channel, particularly when they had Swordfishes. Compared to that our losses were very light. On the typical raid our particular squadron wouldn't lose any, or perhaps one. Other squadrons weren't so lucky.

Did you feel a lot of our equipment was inferior?

I'm afraid it was. In many ways the American stuff was inferior to the Japanese. Their Zero was definitely faster than our thing because they didn't bother about armour plate – that was cissy stuff. We had armour plate behind us to stop a bullet coming in from the back, but not the Japs!

Another of the new types introduced into FAA service during the war was the Grumman Wildcat single-seat fighter, called the Martlet by the British.

Ken Roberts flew Martlets from the decks of small escort carriers like HMS *Biter* – former merchant ships designed to close the gap in air cover in mid-Atlantic.

On the *Biter* when I went there I think there were only two straight ringed [RN regular] officers, the Captain and the navigator. Even the Commander was Wavy Navy. The squadron CO would say who's flying, and he got his orders from – well, we called him 'Wings', the Commander (Flying) was his official title. And he would be under the orders of the Captain. In a fighter squadron like ours we always flew with the same people. Couldn't have the same plane always, but my wing man was always the same person. Although I got to know the odd one or two I didn't really get to know the ground crews.

Our tasks were patrolling, antisubmarine things occasionally, but mostly what we called 'umbrella' – go up high and patrol in case of air attack.

On the *Biter* there were only four fighters, Martlets, and the rest were all Swordfish for submarines. We spent a day on, day off, in pairs. We had to be at instant readiness – we had to sit on the wing of the plane, or in the cockpit if we wanted to, and the other two had to be in the ready room so that they could be off in five minutes if we needed to go.

What was the ship herself like?

Being a converted merchant ship, the accommodation was superb. But they hadn't got proper watertight doors – it was just like going to war in a liner. The sister ship of the *Biter* was torpedoed off the coast of Scotland and no one was saved at all. The *Avenger* I think she was called.

In fact both of *Biter*'s sister ships were sunk with terrible loss of life, *Avenger* by a torpedo which detonated her bomb store, and *Dasher* by an accidental explosion on board.

Strictly speaking we weren't supposed to keep diaries [he shows me a diary entry relating to another escort carrier. It reads 'June 5 – buses took us to the *Battler*. My cabin is a deck below the messdeck and should anything happen the chances of escape are nil but why worry?'] Worse still, I got pulled up for it once or twice. In a lot of these things I even put the names of the ships with us, which is all wrong really. I don't know why you shouldn't keep a diary on a ship, though, because if the ship goes down the diary's not going to be found, is it?

Did you have an action station?

We usually had some duty to do in the case of attack, but we didn't have active things to do – it was mainly safety or keeping out of the way.

Did you lose many friends?

We lost an awful lot of people, but not through enemy action. I don't think any of my personal friends were killed by enemy action, not one, and yet out of the thirty who started off in America, I think only three of us were flying at the end of the war. But it wasn't thanks to the enemy, it was thanks to our own foolishness in most cases. It'll never happen to me – that sort of thing.

When you say people were killed by foolishness, what kind of things were they doing?

Well, he [shows me photo] hit the top of a double-decker bus coming in to land up in Scotland. That was negligence. He [another young face] went over the side. Trying to take off. It was far more dangerous taking off than landing. If anything went wrong, you'd had it.

The accidents at a Royal Naval Air Station, HMS *Heron* at Yeovilton, are also vividly recalled by *Harold Richardson*, then an FAA airframe fitter.

You have to realize that with so many inexperienced pilots being rushed through their training there were bound to be a lot of accidents.

To practise for deck landings, they did many hours of circuits and bumps where they came in to land following the signals of an experienced Batsman standing by the runway. The system

entailed touching down, then immediately opening the throttle
to lift away again and round once more. The heavy bumps onto
the runway sometimes had an unlooked-for effect. The oleo leg
of a Seafire really wasn't strong enough to take the continual
pounding onto a concrete runway that some of these raw young
pilots gave it. One leg would bend slightly, and it would retract
easily enough but then not lower. The red light in the cockpit
would stay on – the green light wouldn't appear. The pilot
would fly low near the control tower, obviously asking them to
look at the undercarriage. The good leg would hang half way
down – it couldn't lock down without the other one. The pilot
would dive the aircraft and roll it in an effort to fling the stuck
leg down, but it never happened. It was always a crash landing.
These happened on the grass, not the runway, and it was
always better if it had been raining so that the ground was a
little bit softer.

The ground staff people tended to become a bit callous about
the many crashes.

The Seafire, the Navy's version of R.J. Mitchell's masterpiece, was
another new type – faster than the Martlet, but with a shorter range.
The Martlet's true successor was the Grumman Hellcat, used in the
Far East.

After a while my foreign draft came through and I left England.
I had a tedious two-month journey before arriving in Durban,
then overland to Cape Town and the large Royal Naval Air
Station there, with Table Mountain as a backdrop.

One end of the establishment was used as a base where
squadrons that were to become carrier-borne did their working-up. 896 Squadron were there at the time and were short of
one or two people, so I volunteered to fill one of the vacancies. I
did the return rail trip to Durban where our ship, the escort
carrier HMS *Ameer*, was supposed to be waiting. In the event
Ameer wasn't ready for sea, so the squadron was embarked in
her sister ship HMS *Empress*. We carried out one operation in
the *Empress* before transferring to the *Ameer*. We were based
at Trincomalee in Ceylon, although we also used Colombo
harbour and Madras in India. The form was that a number of

carriers, usually six, would sail from Ceylon with an escort of destroyers and one capital ship, like the *Nelson*, and carry out bomb and rocket attacks across the Bay of Bengal, and all up and down the Malay peninsula, Sumatra and the Andaman and Nicobar Islands. Our aircraft were all Grumman Hellcats. Casualties were few – 896 Squadron lost only two pilots, one of them our CO, killed by a direct anti-aircraft hit at Phuket, off what was then called Siam.

We were actually at sea when we heard that an atomic bomb had been dropped on Japan.

I wasn't tempted to stay in the service at the end of the war. Civilian life seemed a very enticing prospect from within the Navy! Life was not particularly comfortable, accommodation could be spartan, food was often poor, and your personal liberty was very restricted.

I feel a little differently about it all now, but at twenty-two these things seemed very important.

9

SUBMARINERS

Even more than the Fleet Air Arm, the Submarine Service was a Navy within a Navy. Its members shared a sense of pride in its all-volunteer origins, and regarded themselves as a cut above mere surface ship sailors.

Yet they began the war under something of a cloud. One of their newest boats, the 'T' class *Thetis*, had just been lost in an accident in Liverpool Bay, and public opinion had been shocked by the highly-publicized failure to save the men trapped on board.

The fortunes of the Submarine Service reached their nadir in 1939–40, after HMS *Oxley* (its first casualty) was revealed to have been sunk by another British boat, and HMS *Seal* had suffered the ignominy of surrendering to the enemy.

But as the war progressed the British boats began to deliver a steady stream of successes. Indeed, in many ways they formed the Royal Navy's most potent offensive force, capable of operating in restricted waters which surface ships could only enter at their peril.

A large number of submariners were attracted to the life by the informality found on board, and by the heightened interdependence of the crew members, a mistake by any one of whom could kill them all.

Gordon Ward joined the Royal Navy as a stoker, but volunteered almost immediately for submarines.

I had an idea what they'd be like, and a small ship appealed to me rather than a large one. I started off submarine training at HMS *Dolphin*, Gosport; went through the SEA [submerged escape apparatus] tank – the escape tank – and from there we went to Blyth in Northumberland for the practical stuff. They had a small 'U' class boat there, the *Upright*, which we used to do day trips on, and all the while you're doing the theoretical stuff in the classrooms. Then to Rothesay, to an old tub up there called the *Cyclops*, which acted as depot ship for several First World War submarines – our training boats. I went to sea once or twice in the *L.27* and then was drafted to *H.33*, which was a real bucket. It was always leaking, nasty, very primitive. Did lots of training on there, with day runs across to Ireland, for about six months and then I was drafted to stand by a new boat being finished off at Barrow-in-Furness by Vickers – HMS *Sea Rover*, 'S' class. Ocean-going boats they called them. Did all the working-up trials, and my first patrol was on the North Cape, Murmansk, up that area. Terrible.

Three weeks of hell, you could say. Because it was never calm. Mountainous seas. Icy cold. Dreadful. To surface at night off the North Cape and ditch gash – all the day's rubbish, in buckets – was the most horrendous thing you can ever imagine. The boat is doing everything bar standing on its head, and those buckets had got to be handed by hand up the conning tower. If you're the middle man, at which you had to take your turn, you had it from the chap on top of you. You're picking it out of your hair, and just when you're about to hand another one up to him, half a ton of icy water would come down to add to it. That was the most feared order you waited for at night – ditch gash.

We did a three-week patrol and we didn't see a thing, not a thing. I don't think we could have attacked anything even if we'd seen it. It was an initiation run really, to take the boat out and see how we behaved. My brother who was in the cruiser *Sheffield* did the Murmansk run several times – they had to have the off-watch crew out with hammers knocking the ice off to save her from turning turtle. The heavy seas and ice used to flatten boat davits – used to carry the boats away and flatten the davits down to the decks.

How often would you be on the surface?

Just at night. You dived fourteen hours during the day. You could strike a match and it wouldn't light – it would glow red but it wouldn't burn. That's how bad the air was by the end.

The other thing with the air was that the high pressure lines used to leak, and it used to build up a horrific pressure sometimes. It used to nearly take your ears out of your head. When the hatch was opened the officer of the watch went first, then lookout, who used to have to put his arms round the officer's legs to stop him being pulled out when they took the clips off the top lid. Really take him out – he could fly.

Then we came back down to change over batteries and make everything ready to go to the Far East.

We went via Casablanca, Gib., Beirut for a fortnight, and then on to Colombo and round to Trincomalee. That's where we operated from for I suppose nine months, and then we moved on to Fremantle. A patrol used to last roughly three weeks to a month. It would take several days just to get to the patrol area, of course, so we used to travel on the surface as much as we could, being very alert and having to nip down out of sight of aircraft. Because of the long journeys we used to refuel at Exmouth Gulf, right at the north west tip of Oz. The Americans had a little base there with a tanker and a few huts on shore – all the comforts of home, as the Americans do, even there. They had ice cream and all the rest of it, which we never saw. It was a treat to call in there.

The 'S' class had a crew of forty-seven; five officers, six or seven POs and the rest were so many seamen, so many engineer mechanics as we were called then – they changed from stoker to engineer mechanic when they came into submarines. At action stations I was in what they called the pump room, below the control room, and I operated pumps to maintain her trim during an attack – both when we were attacking and when we were being attacked. We got attacked a lot, depth charging. We got a real bad hammering off Sumatra once – thirty-seven charges in all. We were in shallow water and it shifted the main engines, about twenty-five thou. I think, on the beds. They had these enormous bolts every six inches to hold the big diesels down and it shifted them, that's a guide to the sort of shake-up it was. But the Skipper managed to get out of it by creeping gradually in towards shore as far as water would allow, instead of going out to sea as they thought we would. Thirty-six hours we were there. Our engine room temperature, because we had been running on the surface for a couple of hours and the engines were hot, rose to 172 degrees. I lost a stone and a half in weight on that patrol; took me three years to get it back.

What were living conditions like generally?

Primitive. We didn't shave, mainly because – especially in the Far East – fresh water was at a premium. You probably had to share a bowl of water with two or three others, so you couldn't wash very often. We were right in what they called the 'duck's arse', at the stern, that's where our mess was, and there were nine of us in a place half the size of this room. Three on watch all the time, the other six bunking down where they could. Right next to us were the two twenty-foot diesels, with a gangway down the centre, and two enormous four-stage compressors which we used for charging up the air bottles – they were going flat out as soon as you surfaced. The noise was incredible. No ear defenders in those days – I'm a bit mutt and jeff now in one ear.

We had an Irish chef who we used to say was mad. He had a galley which was five foot square, with one cooker. The food was pretty rough. When we left harbour we used to have fresh meat on board, and fresh veg, but the freezing plant was constantly breaking down, so after three days you could chuck the lot overboard. After that the chef had to knock up whatever he could – corned beef that you could pour out of the tin. Paddy, the chef, used to do very well, considering. He had an electric cooker with rails round it to stop the pans toppling off, but if she hit a swell just as she broke surface or something he could lose the lot. If ever you heard a man swear, ten minutes without a break, that was him.

The Irish have got the gift of rhetoric!

He had, he never stopped. And the galley was right next to the wardroom, so of course they used to tell him to be quiet.

Everybody got the same food?

More or less. I think he used to make a bit of a fuss of the officers whenever he could, but it really wasn't much different. Most of the stuff whatever it was came out of a tin. Had to, because it wouldn't keep.

I hate guavas now because we used to get tinned guavas all

the time. That must have been the cheapest thing the Admiralty could find!

Our worst enemy in the Far East was prickly heat, because of the sweating. We all had nothing on except a towel round our waist, which we took off every five or ten minutes or so to wring out.

And that included the officers too?

Oh yes. The Skipper used to wear a sarong. He was twenty-two, fatter than I am now – he looked a right comedian in his sarong, especially when he was bending down at the periscope.

Was he good?

He was all right. We didn't do any great stupendous things like sinking any battleships, but we did our bit. And he got us out of several scrapes, once when I think our navigator made a bit of a mistake when we had to go through the Lombok Straits one night. That was a dreadful place to get through. The current was seven knots so you had to run through on the surface, trimmed down to give a lower profile, engines flat out; and of course the Japs had got gun batteries on either side. This is only second or third hand, by the time it gets down to the engine room [laughs], but I think the navigator made a bit of a mistake and we landed up in the wrong bay. Instead of the channel we ended up somewhere else.

This meant you were in plain view of the shore?

Oh, all the time, so close inshore. But we made it.

We once lost a man overboard near there. We'd gone to gun stations with this coaster, and shells were flying about all over the place. The coaster was on fire, and the Skipper was getting ready to call the action off when an aircraft came over, so we went to diving stations. The gunlayer shouted to the gunnery officer that he still had a round up the spout. He said 'Well, let it go.' So he pulled the trigger. The 3 inch gun recoiled, as they do, just as one of the gun crew – Spud Murphy was his name – was turning round, and it hit him up the arse and knocked him straight over the side. We dived without him, and he had to paddle around I think for twenty-five minutes till we went back and got him. He was a stroppy little sod, but that calmed him down; that really quietened him down considerably. There were people in the water not far from him from the coaster that was on its way down, so I expect he was thinking what sort of reception he was going to get when they picked him up!

When you were in the engine room, what kind of work were you doing?

Well, one of the jobs was to clean the separators. I don't know whether you've ever been on a dairy farm where they separate the cream from the milk – that's what they had. It's a centrifuge. The diesel on board a sub has to be pushed out of the tanks by the introduction of salt water to compensate, so you don't lose anything from that tank – the oil comes out and the seawater goes in, so you're left with a full tank all the time to keep the boat's trim. Any water that gets in, and any filth – there's a lot of dirt in diesel oils – has to be filtered and separated out. A separator had to be cleaned once a watch. You had two of them, of course, so you could change over to the spare while you cleaned the first one. Then you had your readings to take, every hour or half hour, watch the revs . . .

The machinery always worked all right?

Dear me, no. There wasn't a day went by that there wasn't something wrong. You were repairing, repairing, repairing, all the time. Because of use, conditions, not particularly the workmanship because they did their best, but these boats are the most complicated things on earth. There's so much crammed into such a small space – you've got air systems, water systems, oil systems, hydraulics, electrics, and they all run in tandem, all in trunking. And there's valves galore, because nearly every outboard valve has a corresponding inboard valve as a precaution against depth charging, so every day you're repairing something.

Eventually on one patrol from Fremantle we accidentally rammed an Aussie destroyer – or rather they got in our way! We bent twenty feet of the bows back, and that was our lot. We had to come home.

Did you always think you'd get through the war?

Well, I used to get a few little pangs when I shut the lid down, the engine room hatch, just before we put to sea. Had a look round the harbour and wondered if I'd see it again. But then it goes, and you think no more about it. And when you're in a sticky situation and the boat's getting hammered of course you have a word with Him upstairs, quietly. That helps. I'm not a religious person, not strictly speaking, but you do have your moments, when there is something to turn to, and that is it. There's nothing else.

Frank Hardy spent much of his time in the service dealing with the submariner's chief weapon.

I specialized as a torpedo gunlayer – I went to Whale Island, did a gunnery course, and then subsequently to the torpedo school. My job was the loading and firing of the torpedoes – there was five of us in the fore ends including myself, and I was the one that told them what tube to load, having got my orders from the Skipper. He'd say Load One, Three, Five, or whatever it was, and we'd take the torpedoes off the stowage and load them in. As you shut each breech it would light up on the panel in the control room. Then he'd say 'Fire One', or 'Fire Three', or 'Fire Five', and you pressed the button and off she went. It was a compressed-air charge that fired them, and when that went, the light went out again in the control room so they knew she'd gone. Then you reported, 'Torpedo running, sir'.

You'd hear on the intercom the Skipper say, 'How long to target?' And the officer on the 'fruit machine', who knew the running times of the torpedoes, would tell him how long – ten, nine, eight, and so on, then you'd hear it thud! It sounded as though someone had hit the outside of the submarine with a blooming great hammer. Dong! Just like a bell.

Retaliation came in the form of depth charges, which were dropped around the submarine's suspected position in an effort to sink her or force her to the surface.

MRS HARDY: He hasn't told me much, but he said when they were depth charged they might sit on the bottom for thirty-six hours, with the little red light on and literally no noise. If you coughed they reckoned they could pick it up. All these years afterwards, it's only recently that he's started having a good night's sleep. Anything upsets him I know I'm in for a bad night.

FRANK: I don't know how it happened, but one time a depth charge must have exploded underneath us. And of course it put the shafts out of line on the motors. So they put us in the dry dock when we got into Malta, and the centre section was six inches higher than the bow and the stern!

And she still managed to operate?

Yes, they lined up the shafts. One of the chaps painted out the name *Unbroken* and put *Badly Bent* underneath, and the name stuck!

What was Malta like as a base?

Oh, for two years solid – and it wasn't just one day, it was every day and night on Malta – we were bombed by the Italian Air Force, and also by the Germans. When we was in port we used to have to take the sub from the side of the creek out into the middle of the harbour and dive her during the day so she wouldn't be seen, and come up at night time. I don't know how the Maltese people stood it, because that place was an absolute ruin by the time they'd finished.

We had a battery fire out in the Med. once. The battery's all under the floor, twenty-eight tons of it, and we had one of the cells catch fire. Of course it just filled the whole of the interior of the submarine with yellowish-brown smoke. And when we came into Grand Harbour it looked as if we were steaming in because we had the conning tower hatch open and everybody on deck! There was this great plume of smoke coming out. The blokes who were in the engine room were working with Davis escape apparatus on.

Did you get much leave?

When I was at home over here, yes. Many a time we'd get home to Rosyth and the Skipper would say 'There's a train leaving Waverley Station at midnight – if you can make it, away you go!', and he'd give us each a pass. I remember once I just barely made it. Got me old ditty box on, into the compartment, and it's just got the little blue lights. Slung it up on the luggage rack, and I got up there with it. I woke up about Durham. I could hear grunting and groaning down below and I looked down, and there's this Bootneck with his girlfriend, wasn't he? Blimey, wasn't I glad when York station comes and they got out! I daren't say a word! What they were doing was nobody's business. Cor, all the way down to York from Durham! He'd have killed me!

10

BOOTNECKS

All of the larger warships in the fleet carried a complement of Royal Marines, who could be put ashore if circumstances required a show of force. When on board they helped to man some of the ship's weapons, including one of the main gun turrets, and also carried out the unspoken function of restraining any potential indiscipline on the part of the seamen or stokers. 'Protecting the officers from the crew', as one seaman laughingly put it.

The Royal Marines had a distinct identity, quite separate from the Navy. This special position was emphasized both by their traditions and by the regulations which governed their daily lives. For example, Royal Marine barracks flew the Union Flag rather than the White Ensign, since they were not commissioned as ships like naval shore establishments; their rank structure was that of the Army, not the Navy; and they were subject to the Naval Discipline Act afloat but the Army Act ashore (the dividing line being the ship's gangway).

Harry Usher joined this elite Corps in 1935, as a band boy.

At that time conditions hadn't changed much since Kipling's day. We still had two choices at meal times – take it or leave it! But having come from a Royal Marines background I was proud to wear the uniform.

I was seventeen and a half when I joined HMS *Kent*, which commissioned at Chatham in June 1938 as flagship of the China Squadron. A commission at that time lasted about two and a half years.

We arrived in Hong Kong some six weeks later. The band's

duties were mainly ceremonial – we played for wardroom guest nights, entertained the lower deck and provided the music for funerals and other functions.

What were your officers like?

The pre-war ones, apart from a few rankers, were a race apart. They had nothing in common socially with the men. At the same time they always looked after the mens' welfare, and they were respected. They were very paternalistic, and always had our best interests at heart. Looking back I can see that the pre-war Navy was very racist, though had we been told so at the time we wouldn't have understood the meaning of the word. We just took it for granted that the British were better than anyone else. I remember being told at school that one Englishman was worth three foreigners! I recall the case of a young marine who wanted to marry a Hong Kong Chinese girl – respectable, I might add. His officer tried to talk him out of it, but to no avail. He was on the next ship returning to England. Everyone agreed it was for his own good.

After more than a year of peacetime service on the China Station, war broke out back in Europe and the *Kent* was moved to Ceylon.

We ranged around the Indian Ocean for a while, then down to Perth, Australia to escort Australian troop transports as far as Cape Town on their way to the Middle East. Our next move was to the Mediterranean, where we joined the fleet at Alexandria.

We patrolled the Aegean Sea and then, in mid-September 1940, we set out for a night bombardment of Bardia, on the coast of North Africa. During this action, when all hands were concentrating on the coastline, an Italian torpedo bomber managed to sneak up from seaward and put a tin fish into our port quarter.

The ship came to a halt and heeled over to port; the lights went out and an eerie silence ensued. The band's action station was in the transmitting station, a room in the bowels of the ship which fed information to the guns. We just sat and prayed that the ship wouldn't capsize, because if she had we would have drowned like rats. There was no question of us getting to the upper deck – the TS hatch could only be opened from above.

After what seemed like an age they finally allowed us up. The TS, being a vital watertight compartment, had to remain sealed until it was ascertained that the ship wasn't going to sink – the safety of the ship being paramount.

The destroyer *Nubian* took us in tow and we eventually made it back to Alexandria. After temporary repairs we limped home to Plymouth round the Cape. Thus ended my first commission!

With the *Kent* out of action for a whole year, Harry was drafted to another County class cruiser, HMS *Shropshire*. He later served aboard the battleship *Resolution*, and finished the war in the auxiliary *Menestheus*, which sailed under the Red Ensign of the British merchant fleet.

The *Menestheus* was unique, she was an old Blue Funnel liner converted into a floating brewery. Her holds contained large tanks where seawater was distilled into fresh, and with the addition of various chemicals a passable bitter could be brewed. She also carried a concert party and a first class RM orchestra. It was intended that she should join the fleet train of the British Pacific Fleet as an amenity ship, but by the time we got to the Far East the atomic bombs had been dropped and the war was over. As far as I know, no other Navy possessed such a vessel!

In addition to their traditional roles, the Royal Marines were given a historic new responsibility in mid-war. From 1943 they were given control of the burgeoning fleet of minor landing craft needed for amphibious operations. The Coxswain of one such craft, HM *LCM. 1144*, was *Arthur Burns*, who joined the Marines just when this changeover was being implemented.

Basic training was an initial eight weeks at Chatham barracks, now demolished. It consisted mainly of drill on the square, with one daily period of PT and about one weekly period of bayonet practice; nothing else. Much emphasis was placed on the drill, the MTIs [Military Training Instructors] being so steeped in it that their whole being was wrapped up in turning the forty-strong squad into a thing of beauty, from the barrack square viewpoint. While we were there a new King's Squad passed out. This was a crack squad whose drill was something to marvel at; it included fixing bayonets on the march, which was something of a show-stopper!

Training continued at Walmer, with the nitty-gritty of soldiering; route marches, bivouacking, instruction on the Bren and other weapons, and more PT.

Then came Combined Operations, since the Marines had taken over all the minor landing craft from the Navy. This was said to have been decided because the Marines' greater discipline was desirable when in small groups such as individual boats' crews of six – Coxswain, Stoker and four deck hands.

Training commenced on LCAs [Landing Craft, Assault] at Clacton, continued at Felixstowe where we picked up our LCMs [Landing Craft, Mechanized], and finished at Itchenor near Chichester, from where we sailed for Normandy with the 652nd LCM Flotilla.

Our LCM was a landing craft capable of carrying anything up to a DUKW [amphibious truck] in size, with a tall square steel box aft for the Coxswain. Two major faults with them were the difficulty in starting the twin diesel engines on cold mornings and the noise they made when travelling at even moderate speed. Neither of these aspects was a problem with what were known as 'British' LCMs, which had quiet petrol engines. Our LCMs were built in America, or so we understood.

We found the actual training on the LCMs quite pleasant during the summer months, but frequently rather less so in the winter, especially when tidal conditions made night operations necessary. Tides were actually a constant problem, especially at one place on the east coast where the rise and fall were extreme.

The eighteen craft of the flotilla were tied up there along a sea wall, and it was a sentry's duty to keep them as close to it as possible during the night. On an incoming tide this was easy; the sentry merely had to stroll along the line, hauling in each rope as it slackened. On a falling tide, however, the drop was so rapid that it was all he could do to race along the line, letting out each rope before it became taut. At the end of the line he literally had to run back to the beginning and start again. On one occasion he didn't make it in time – the rope was taut round the ring on the wall, couldn't be budged and ended up taking the steadily increasing weight of the LCM as it went down with the tide. In a panic he cut the rope, without first taking the precaution of securing the LCM with another one; of course down it went with a splash, and then started drifting out to sea. More panic! The crew of another craft had to be hurriedly got out of bed to chase after the 'escapee'. That crew was mine, and although we were soon away, the night had swallowed up our quarry completely so that we located it only after allowing ourselves to be carried down by the same falling tide, assisted by occasional bursts of engine power. We eventually caught it up, lassoed it and brought it triumphantly home again. After that, two sentries were on duty every night!

In June 1944 the 652nd Flotilla found itself allocated to the JUNO landing area, the central of the three British sectors.

Security was in fact excellent. Not until the evening of our departure were we told we were off to Normandy. It was when we began butting into the waves that we realized we were in trouble. During our training we had been plagued with engine and other defects in the LCMs, but in the preceding few weeks the artificers had worked like slaves on them so that when we set off the craft were in better shape than they had ever been. In the case of my boat, however, an omission became evident – the packing in the hinge of the ramp hadn't been checked. In were coming small spurts of water that quickly flooded the well deck, and with it our kitbags and lashed hammocks which had been stowed there. This was bad enough, but when these items, washing back and forth, repeatedly hit against sixty five-gallon cans of diesel that had been lashed together at the after end of the well deck, these eventually broke free, tumbled over and emptied their contents. The smell of 300 gallons of diesel, albeit mixed with sea water, was indescribable and those of us who had defied the rough weather till then soon succumbed to seasickness. It was a somewhat sorry crew who somehow managed to hold our bucking bronco of a boat more or less in position all the way over to France.

Once there, the LCMs and other landing craft were kept busy ferrying munitions, food and fuel to the invasion beaches from the cargo ships anchored offshore.

On occasion we were also roped in to perform sentry duty on the beach at night, and as this meant moving to an area well away from our boats, we dug two-man bivouacs in the sand, from which we emerged to do two hours on, two off. One night was windy and we dug our bivouac under the lee of a large bank of sand at the head of the beach. What a mistake! I was on duty first, so left my oppo getting his head down while I wandered off with my rifle slung over my shoulder ready to repel all those German soldiers who would be creeping along the beach to murder us all while we slept – or something. I'd gone but ten yards when I thought I heard a call. I hesitated, but finally went back to the bivouac, to find my oppo had been virtually buried by a fall of sand, from which I extricated him just in time for a further fall to cover him again and myself also, up to the knees. More furious digging and he emerged – sand in his ears, nose and mouth but otherwise OK!

After some six weeks of ferrying our LCMs began one by one to suffer various breakdowns, both in engines and because of structural damage caused by the continual storms that summer. By that time PLUTO [Pipe Line Under The Ocean] was in operation, pumping fuel right across the Channel direct to the beaches, and so our usefulness had come to an end and we were ordered home to the UK. There was no possibility of returning under our own power and so, two craft at a time, we were somewhat ignominiously towed behind an LCT [Landing craft, Tank], this being a bigger landing craft, skippered by a naval Lieutenant.

Once again heavy weather was in evidence, and before long the ropes between our two craft parted. The tow rope from the LCT was attached to us, so the other LCM drifted off. Fortunately one of his two engines still operated and he was able to crawl back to us while the LCT hove to. We made fast again but it was the same story, until the final blow came when the tow rope, fastened to a cleat on the port side close to the ramp, slackened for an instant and then made an almighty snatch when it tightened again, pulling the cleat clean out of its mounting.

The ramp was held in place by means of a stout wire rope wound round a hand-operated winch at the after end, this wire running along the port side above the catwalk. The cleat, pulled forward with great force, became entangled with the wire and struck the edge of the ramp with a solid thud. Instantly there was a sound of tearing metal from the winch, which was welded to the metal deck by two flanges of a steel platform it was fixed to, and in the twinkling of an eye the winch and its platform hurtled forward, smashing a fire extinguisher out of its securing lugs, and straight overboard. Released from its restraining wire rope, down went the ramp with a splash, and in about five minutes the well deck was awash.

The tow rope, with cleat still attached, had pulled clear as the ramp fell and so the LCT stopped again. Unaccountably, however, it did not turn back to us, although the difficulties we were now in, with the ramp hanging down into the sea and thus effectively preventing any forward motion, were obvious. The reason was soon revealed; the LCTs signaller semaphored the message to us that we had drifted into a minefield.

No sooner was this known when, as if to prove that the LCT Skipper knew what he was talking about, there on the port bow about thirty to forty yards off was the unmistakable shape of a sea mine, evidently anchored just below the surface and only revealed in between big waves. The 'horns' of the mine, as seen in many a film were plainly in view and galvanized the Coxswain of the other LCM into action. He frantically restarted the one engine he possessed and at full revs he moved off, taking us with him in a circle! The ramp on my LCM was the obstacle to moving forward; although the other boat's wheel was hard over to port to counter our drag on its starboard side, the one engine was unequal to the task of pulling the two boats along. The other LCM was in fact closest to the mine, and its Coxswain was so mesmerized by it that he could think of nothing but keeping his engine going full blast, despite our two boats going nowhere but in a tight circle. Eventually someone ran up to him and told him to go astern as the only way to get clear.

This did the trick and with infinite slowness we crept away, finally reaching the LCT.

By this time, however, the LCT Skipper had had enough. After more than three hours the Normandy coast was still well in sight, so we were told to abandon ship and go aboard the LCT. Being fed up ourselves we were very pleased to do so. What was to become of the two derelicts, however? No problem as far as the extrovert Skipper of the LCT was concerned – he would sink them, giving his two oerlikon gunners some useful target practice in the process. Accordingly, both guns let fly and as tracers were included we were able to watch fascinated as a hail of heavy bullets thudded into the two boats, above and below the waterline. They did not, nevertheless, sink; doubtless due to their below deck construction being a series of watertight compartments, only the outer ones of which were presumably holed by the gunfire.

We moved slowly away and ceased firing only when out of range, leaving the two boats still tossing up and down. We watched till they were out sight – and I have often wondered what their ultimate end could have been. To whoever came across them it must have seemed like a modern-day *Marie Celeste*, and I just hoped that whoever did meet up with them didn't do so at night. I've said that the Skipper was an extrovert and we all just assumed that we were sailing away from this potential hazard without a care, but on reflection as a presumably responsible naval officer he might well have sent a general warning message by radio to all ships.

With hindsight, the best method of towing the two boats would have been by way of a main tow rope to one LCM, with a secondary one from that boat to the other one astern of it, thus avoiding the interaction between the two when lashed alongside each other. No one thought of that at the time, however, and certainly no one could have imagined that a cleat would have been pulled right out of its mounting.

This time everything seemed set fair; the weather eased, the sun shone and we all lounged around on deck, idly watching the LCT Skipper taking pot shots with a pistol at empty bottles heaved overboard at the bows as they floated past the bridge at the stern. This was when the odd passing sea bird was not being shot at! For a Royal Navy officer that Lieutenant was a bit of a character, as many of the wartime ones were.

The call for 'grub up' at midday had just been made, and some of us had already moved off to the mess, when perhaps the biggest fright of my life occurred. Absolutely out of the blue a lone German plane came swooping down on us, machine guns blazing. The speed with which the plane dived was too great for most of us to even get under cover, and it was only by the greatest good fortune that no one was hit. There was just the one short burst of gunfire and the plane was over, apparently only a few feet above us, and then away, climbing steeply and swiftly vanishing from sight.

Fright gave way to anger that we had been so taken by surprise, especially as a member of the LCT crew was on the bridge as lookout. That man was suitably chastened, but explained that although he was keeping watch, it was on the sea rather than in the air. To some extent this was understandable because enemy planes had been notably absent the whole time we had been in France; this one adopted the classic aerial warfare tactic of diving on us out of the sun, a manoeuvre that dates back to the earliest dog fights and is still effective today – or at least was in 1944.

Looking at the damage caused by the few hits made on the LCT by the plane's guns, we were thankful none of us had been hit; little imagination was necessary to envisage the carnage such firepower would have caused. The hits were all above the waterline, so we carried on and reached Portsmouth with no further mishap – with all of us becoming volunteer lookouts for the remainder of the trip!

I I

WRNS

Although the Admiralty had seen no need for servicewomen in peacetime, the run-up to war brought increasing pressure on them to repeat their First World War experiment of establishing an all-female branch to release men for sea. The Women's Royal Naval Service (WRNS) was formally re-established under its First World War title in April 1939 – the only one of the three women's services to retain its old name.

It was originally envisaged that WRNS personnel, universally known as 'Wrens' regardless of rank, would only be employed ashore. But the range of jobs grew as quickly as the service itself, and many of them did in fact serve afloat as crews for harbour launches or as boarding officers at ports and convoy assembly points. After D-Day Wrens were routinely employed on the cross-Channel shuttle service.

Eventually eighty or so categories were filled by them. Of these, the largest proportion were in the domestic field – like cooks and stewards – but there were also Wren cypher officers, telegraphists, meteorologists, ship mechanics (trained in the repair and mainten-ance of landing craft) and a host of other specialist trades.

There were initially two levels of service, rather inelegantly termed 'Mobile' and 'Immobile'. Mobile Wrens could be drafted to any base, and were housed in quarters. Immobile Wrens, like *Anne Partridge*, lived at home and engaged only to serve at their nearest base.

We lived in Torpoint, a small town right opposite the naval dockyard at Devonport, so ships had always been a part of our lives. During the early war years Wrens could serve either as Mobile or Immobile – in the latter category service was only to be in one's home base. Since all my male family were away at sea I chose to be Immobile, so worked at Plymouth.

Training with the WRNS was very brief – in 1940, when I joined, the war was hotting up. We did our share of square-bashing, instructed by a fierce Chief Gunnery Instructor who didn't consider us capable of marching but was determined to lick us into shape somehow.

Being an officer's steward – cleaning shoes, serving meals and working in the wardroom bar – wasn't my idea of essential war work, so in 1941 when the Admiralty asked for volunteers from serving Wrens to be trained as boats' crews to man harbour launches I put in for it. I was one of the first six Wrens to serve afloat. After a short training in knots, signals and semaphore we were drafted to two little hospital boats, *Nightingale* and *Cavell*. We worked alternate twenty-four hour watches, sleeping in hammocks. Eventually most of the harbour launches were manned by Wrens.

Hospital boats were used for various duties – fetching casualties from ships, sometimes ferrying prisoners of war, mainly from U-boats, from the ships which had picked them up. Quite often we were used as tenders to destroyers and cruisers, carrying mail out and bringing libertymen in for a run ashore.

When we went into boats' crews we were each issued with oilskins, sou'wester, seaboots, men's bell bottom trousers, lanyard, knife and a hammock. Initially the Admiralty considered it 'unseemly' for Wrens to walk through the streets in bell bottoms, so we had to wear our skirts going to and from duty, changing into trousers on our boats. Since we were often tied up alongside destroyers you can perhaps imagine the hilarity caused by the sight of Wrens in skirts and stockings climbing over guard rails. Finally we got permission to wear trousers going to and from boat duty, but nowhere else! How fashions have changed since then.

Most Wrens, however, served in various capacities on shore. *Eileen Woolley* was trained in one of the signals specializations.

It was a comparatively small service when I volunteered, and it must have been at least six months or more before I was called. I was sent to Plymouth to do my fortnight's probationary training, and thence to HMS *Heron*, the Naval Air Station at Yeovilton. After a week there I was posted to the satellite field at Charlton Horethorne, near Sherborne; affectionately known as 'Charlie H'.

You can imagine the shock of a girl brought up in Lee in the suburbs south of London, suddenly finding herself miles from anywhere in the depths of the countryside, with just a few Nissen huts in the middle of a field.

At Charlie H I was a signals distibution office watchkeeper, and at first went into Yeovilton every day to learn my job, which really consisted of receiving and sending signals about aircraft movements, stores, and so on. When signals arrived by teleprinter and were passed to me I had to decide who on the camp needed to know, get the appropriate copies typed and send them out by messenger – on a bike! – to the various people. When I first decided to become an SDO watchkeeper I fancied I'd be on a cliff sending out signals to ships, but in reality a lot of SDOs at big naval bases were underground. I was bored stiff on duty as so few signals came in. But after a year, when I went back to Yeovilton, I was always busy and the time passed much quicker.

Of course we stood watches, which as far as I can remember were on a four-day cycle. We weren't very popular with the stewards who cleaned the cabin, because there would always be a few 'bods' in bed, and they took great delight in banging brooms against our bunks to wake us up. However, being watchkeepers also meant we managed to get out of most of the squarebashing that went on – most of us would very conveniently be 'on duty', and so unavailable. We did do some, though, and I can't say it worried me much. It was quite enjoyable at times to feel part of a team.

I was also lucky with food, because my best friend – then and now – had married a local farmer, so when I came off night duty I would cycle to their cottage, where there were always plenty of eggs and bacon. Cyril would go and shoot a rabbit if Mary hadn't much food, and there was cream and milk, so I suppose that's why I haven't any memories of camp food – I was well fed elsewhere!

The airfield at Charlie H was just grass fields, and as the hills dropped away suddenly it was rather like taking off from a carrier, or so I imagine. We had three squadrons there, 780, 790 and 794. On my twenty-first birthday in 1944 I was allowed to fly with 790 Squadron in a Fairey Fulmar, and I have a photograph of myself in flying gear having just landed. Though it's quite a good job the photo is black and white, and doesn't show my delicate green colour!

Like all WRNS officers, *Phyllis Hansell* had joined as a Wren and had been selected for officer training at the Royal Naval College, Greenwich.

I was at Greenwich during the buzz bombs. We had a bit of naval history, lectures, and a bit of law. We had to write essays and give an impromptu speech on anything we liked – I did first aid because I'd been in the Red Cross and the Civil Nursing Reserve. And each week we had a test on what we'd learned, written essays. Squad drill, and PT.

You were chosen to be officers. You worked your way up to it.

Do you know what they decided that on, what they were looking for?

Oh, I think whether you were good at your job, whether you had power of command, whether you mixed well – whether you were amenable to discipline.

In fact there was very little indiscipline, only one girl – we had right at the top of this hotel a little hut which was for the visual signallers, who had to be up there twenty-four hours a day, as it was the only means of communicating with the ships. They had two on at night and they changed shifts. Well, about half past eight one morning a steward came to me and she said, 'I hate to tell anything on anybody, but Bambi' – she was known as that because she was tiny, very pretty – 'was on the half past six ferry going off to the mainland, and she was on duty here till eight.' She said 'It feels like sneaking, but' she said 'it only left one Wren up there.' I said 'Don't worry'. I sent for the Leading Wren and told her; she was horrorstruck. Then I sent for the other girl who had stayed on duty, and asked her what time she'd come off. 'Eight o'clock ma'am'. What time had Bambi come off? 'Eight o'clock ma'am'. So I said 'You're lying, you know'. She burst into tears. I said 'Bambi left, didn't she?' 'Yes ma'am, at six o'clock'. And she'd beetled down to catch the half past six ferry. This kid was on a two-day leave, so I told the people on the front door of the hotel that when she came back she was to come straight up to me. She had to come before the Captain, and he gave her thirty days pay stopped plus the loss of thirty days leave.

What was the attitude of the men in the RN to you?

They accepted us, but not to begin with I believe. The die-hards, they thought this was ghastly. We didn't see much of the ratings. We did get to know the officers – one was only twenty-five, and his CO was in his early thirties. We played bridge with them when they were there, but that was all.

Did you get a tot of rum like the men?

VE-Day was the only time I ever tasted rum! Wrens didn't receive a tot, but we were a mixed station, so when the Captain gave the order to splice the mainbrace you could hardly leave the Wren officers out.

What about accommodation, at the various shore bases?

Generally the Navy took over big old houses for us. If you lived in dispersed quarters, as they were known, at eight o'clock at night you got on a lorry and it took you back there, and brought you in in the morning.

Were many of the Wrens married?

Yes, there were one or two. And one or two widows – who'd lost their husbands in the Navy, and had joined up themselves.

Did you enjoy your time in the service?

I wouldn't have missed it. Somebody wrote later that it widened your way of thinking and the whole mode of life. But of course when you came back, parents never realized what you'd done and the responsibility. I remember my father saying to me, 'Where are you going? What time will you be home?' And I just looked at him in astonishment.

Many young Wrens, like *Monica Moxley*, found that the life could be almost idyllic if they were drafted to the right spot.

I joined the WRNS in 1942, and after training as a cinema operator I was sent off to the Royal Marine Military School at Thurlestone. I found a note waiting for me in my letter rack telling me to go 'by own steam to Paddington Station', then to catch a train to Newton Abbot, change to another train to South Brent, and another to Kingsbridge, where I would be met!

I set off in my new uniform with my suitcase to Paddington – I had never travelled on my own before, except on local trains. I produced my pass and found a seat on the crowded train mostly packed with sailors. It was one thirty and lunch was being served on the train, so I sat in the restaurant car and started my lunch while we were still in the station. Eventually there was a great snorting of steam, and we were on our way to the West. When we finally arrived at Newton Abbot I had to wait some time for the next train to take me to South Brent, and a train full of soldiers steamed slowly through the station, the men calling out 'Hiya Jack' to the sailors. Great fun. At long last the next train chugged in and I found a corner seat, which was as well, as I was able to look out at the countryside for the next few hours that train took to make the fairly short journey. After a further train I arrived at Kingsbridge Station, where I was met by a Captain of the Royal Marines and a Wren officer. I was told to jump into the rear of the jeep, and we drove along the narrow lanes to Thurlestone. I was taken to the orderly office and told where my cabin was. Having unpacked my case I couldn't resist walking out of the french windows of the sunroom which was to be my home, and across the grass to the top of the cliffs.

It was October when I first arrived there, and one would have thought it was still summer, so I spent my off duty time on the beach. Our work wasn't very demanding, showing the odd instructional film during the day, and entertainment films on the first three evenings of each week.

During the spring we went for country walks. Sometimes I would take an empty container and collect wild flowers – I packed these posies in damp moss in a tin and sent them home; my mother said they arrived the next morning with the dew still on them as if they had just been picked.

It would become very hot in our cabin at night; there were ten people in five double bunks. The blackout arrangements had to be a good fit, no chink of light was allowed, so it was a great relief when the last person to go to bed took this blackout cover down, and we all felt we could breathe.

There were many men passing through the Military School. It was a very tough course, and a lot of them slept during the instructional films. One of the training officers, a Major, had a saying as he sent the men off on the last exercise of the course, 'The colder the night, the wetter the night, he darker the night, the *better* the night!' Off they went in trucks to be dropped in the heart of Dartmoor to find their own way back. Those that had passed the course then went straight to a passing out parade, nearly dead in their boots. The others would perhaps get drunk. That night there was a dance, and great jollification, but in reality they were off to the war perhaps never to return, such young enthusiastic boys of eighteen years or so.

12

SURVIVORS

There can be few events more traumatic for a sailor than that of losing his ship. A sense of helplessness, plus regret over the loss of possessions and, in many cases, the death of shipmates are the commonest emotions expressed by those who have gone through the experience.

Some men, particularly in the Merchant Navy, were unlucky enough to experience it several times during their war service.

One of the most famous sinkings was that of the aircraft carrier *Ark Royal*, returning from a successful operation in the Mediterranean. *Alfred Pizer* was a telegraphist/air gunner in one of her squadrons.

I was in the *Ark* for a year including the sinking of the *Bismarck*, and then on 13 November 1941 we were sunk ourselves. My favourite story of that was when I came home the local paper came round to see me, and I said when the Captain gave the order to abandon ship, I still don't know who the second man was off the ship!

We were eighteen miles outside of Gibraltar when a German submarine hit us with two torpedoes. As aircrew we were the first off the ship – we were told we were useless. They tried to tow her into port but it was very, very windy; it was in November you see, and she sank the next morning. There was no panic rush to get off. She listed right over, but there was no panic. Except for me! In fact it took several hours before they decided to say, 'abandon ship'. Destroyers came alongside and we lowered rope ladders, and you climbed down them on to the deck of the destroyer.

Hitler kept on saying all through 1940 'The *Ark Royal* has been sunk', 'the *Ark Royal* has been sunk', all during 1941, 'The *Ark Royal* has been sunk'. When the ship *was* sunk, another thing that was funny – we were called survivors; there were fifteen hundred crew at the time, and only one man was killed, and yet we were all called survivors, the fourteen hundred and ninety-nine!

But few stricken ships remained afloat for over fourteen hours, as did the *Ark Royal*. Many, like the battleship *Barham*, went down in minutes. Stoker *Arthur Francis* was one of the handful of survivors from the *Barham*, whose loss claimed the lives of 848 officers and men from her ship's company.

My first draft when I finished my training was called Med. disposal, and it was true – they disposed of nearly all of us. We were detailed, party of about twenty or thirty of us, several days to go on board HMS *Barham*. They took us out in a launch, and we had to go down to the engine room and clean up or paint the lagging or something under the watchful eye of a PO. This PO, he used to say to us, if you do a good job I'll get you a transfer, a draft, because this ship's unsinkable. This is true! He said we've got a bomb-proof upper deck, torpedo bulges at the sides, all the way down; she's unsinkable.

Sure enough we got sent to the *Barham* after a couple of weeks, because she'd been away from England for a couple of years and a lot of them were due back. We three with the consecutive service numbers – Fisher, Francis and Fenn – went in the same mess, No.7 Mess, but after she was sunk there was only me. That's the tragic bit about it, they only lived at Rainham, just about four miles up the road from me, and when we met during the training period, before we went abroad, our families got very close. When we were sunk in the November of 1941 they sent the two wives, Fisher's wife and Fenn's wife, a letter expressing their regret that their husband had been lost at sea. Of course they jumped on a bus and flew round to my wife, and found her round my parents' house in Romford. Lots of tears, naturally, and of course my wife was frightened to go home because there'd probably be a letter on the mat for her too.

Rotten old thing it was, *Barham*. Loathed it. Apparently she was built during the First World War, and she was the only one of her class that hadn't been refitted. She wasn't built for the climate out in the Eastern Mediterranean; ventilation was atrocious.

On a battleship you have a regulating Chief Stoker in the Engine Room Branch, and he sits in his little caboosh and details all the duties – who's going to do what. When we joined the *Barham*, we went back to the mess and the old sweats in the mess said 'What you got?' I said I've got auxiliary watch-keeping. 'Who are you with?' I said 'Chief Stoker Ludlow'. 'Kin 'ell', they said, 'he's mad! Nobody sticks him!' I thought oh well, you know [laughs]. So true enough he was barmy. He didn't know what home was – he'd joined as a boy and he was forty odd by now. He would have been out but for the war. When we went to sea he went down the boiler room in charge, and I went with him.

This particular day we had the morning watch, which is four in the morning till eight, and nobody likes being woken up at quarter to four in the morning, do they? Particularly him! He really led me a dog's life. No peace – the sweat was running off me, and getting towards eight o'clock he gave me one last job to do that was a real bastard, you know, so I said something to him. He said he'd have me up in front of the regulating chief. I said 'Listen, I'm already going there as soon as we go up, but if you want to come with me you're welcome!' With that our relief came down and we went up. True enough, I didn't even go and change or anything. I was fuming. When I got to the Chief I said I wanted a change. 'Who are you with?' I said 'Ludlow'. 'How long you been with him?' I said 'three months!' 'Cor blimey, that's the longest anybody's ever stayed with him!' He said 'Hang on a minute.' Sheets of paper. 'You've got a Stoker in your mess named Jameson? Well tell him to pick up from your first dog watch and you do his last dog in a different boiler room. Tell him he can come and see me if he's got any problems.' Just that very day, and at twenty-five past four we were sunk, so it should have been me really.

Me and Len Fisher were sitting in the mess together when it happened. There was a bang and a shudder, and old Len said, green as grass, 'I wonder what that is?' All the bleeding lights went out, crockery broke, little secondary lighting came on, dim, and then there was another one. I said we'd better go up and have a look. We were three decks down, our messdeck, so we went up the first ladder, then the second one, and I could tell she was listing then because we had a problem to go up the ladders. And then she shook again, and I thought bloody hell! When we got to the upper deck she was really listing over, and we had to go uphill. I could see 'em all jumping in, and don't forget from the time we were first hit till she disappeared was only three and a half minutes so things were a bit hectic. My friend Len couldn't swim. We slid down the ship's side to the torpedo bulge, and I said well, what you gonna do? I looked at him and I could see terror – his eyes were staring and I knew that he was very, very frightened. The water was just abhorrent to him. He only had this inflated inner tube thing. I said come on then, because we were right level with the water – we only had to step in – when all of a sudden, bang! Us being right down there saved us as she turned right over and tipped us on our backs, into the water. I could just see Len's feet near my eyes as we hit the water, and when I came up I felt a hand round my ankle once, but there wasn't much I could do. I couldn't see a thing, I thought well, either I'm blind or she's floating upside down. Stupid thing, I know, but that's what I thought. But it was all bloody smoke, and when it cleared I could see wreckage, and oil, all black with oil. On the lockers, where they used to sit, they had these flat cushions about that thick, shiny ones. One of these about that long was right near so I got hold of it. I thought, well, nobody near me but I've only got to swim a little way and there they are. And in the distance two little masts – two destroyers – so I knew they were coming back for us. Out of nowhere came this guy, swimming, and under his arm he had a bloke's head. Then I saw the body was with it, and the guy said 'Can I put my oppo on your cushion, mate?' I said 'yeah', and we dropped him on it – he was out cold – but the bloody thing sank. He said, 'Hang on, hold my mate, will you?' I said 'yeah', because I was a good swimmer, while he swam away and got a great long length of the ship's cutter, about from here to that wall, all jagged. He held one end and I held the other, and we propped his mate over the middle. Trouble was, with the swell the thing was twisting, and in the end we had to let it go, and down he went. Round comes his mate, props him up again; whenever he went he'd pick him up. He was still out. I thought to myself he's wasting his time.

We were all black, thick black oil, but finally they started picking up. Two destroyers, one was the *Hotspur* and the other one, the one I got on, was the Australian *Nizam*. We were the last because all the others were nearer. I said to him I think we'd better attract somebody's attention, because it looked as though they were finished, so when they did come over they said good job you waved, we didn't know there was any more – couldn't see you.

I climbed up the scrambling net, and the Chief up there said as you go through the bulkhead, mate, there's a PO with some rum – that's the first thing. Then there's the bathroom, because you've got to get rid of all this oil. I only had overalls on, chucked 'em off and somebody gave me a blanket. 'Who are you, seaman or stoker?' – because there's segregation. I said 'stoker'. 'Go down the stokers' mess deck.'

Next morning I must admit we were all feeling sorry for ourselves, because realization has suddenly hit you. And the throb of the engines during the night. It's all running through your mind. I went up on the upper deck. One bloke had died during the night, survivor, and they buried him at sea. We all wanted to attend that. We didn't have to, we really wanted to. Then I just sat there on my own, looking at the water. And two guys came walking along – it was this bloke and his mate! Shook hands with me. I didn't know him, because on a big ship you didn't know 'em all. He said, 'I was just telling my mate somebody helped me – I'm glad I met you!'

The attack on the *Barham* demonstrated the alarming vulnerability of the big ships, even with a destroyer screen. Coming as it did just eleven days after the sinking of the *Ark Royal*, the decision was taken to suppress the news for reasons of morale. Only months afterwards did the Admiralty officially admit her loss.

After being picked up and taken back to Alexandria, they sent us to an air station to rest and get over it, and then they said there's a couple of quid, you can have forty-eight hours leave. But you mustn't try and contact home at all; you're very hush-hush; just go and get drunk.

So he went to see his brother, serving in Egypt with the Army.

In January I was in Cape Town on my way home, and I went ashore on a Saturday evening – January is the middle of their summer, beautiful – and I was making my way to the local bar. I bought an evening paper, and there it was, 'HMS *Barham* sunk'; but two months after. And the wife actually saw it later at the pictures, you know, used to have the Pathe News and that.

Eventually I landed back home in March, middle of March. I had a fortnight's leave, then reported back at Chatham.

All these ships that you got were normally manned by one port division – it's a Chatham ship, or a Pompey ship, or a Devonport ship, and everybody's from that same manning port. But during wartime I went on the *Barham* and it was a Pompey ship although I was a Chatham rating. OK, it didn't make any difference to the war effort, but when the *Barham* was sunk apparently it was an extremely black day in Pompey. Yet when I arrived back in March, back to Chatham, they said 'Where?' 'Who?' So I was promptly shipped to a destroyer, but some of them survivors from Pompey never went to sea again! It was – oh, better not send him, he's a survivor off the *Barham*.

There was only two of us out of the original class that joined up at Skegness that came back, a little Scotsman and me, and funnily enough he couldn't swim a stroke.

If something like that happened today, at least there'd be counselling.

Ah, no. All these things go by the board when there's a war on; nobody cares as long as the war's being fought, that's the main thing. And if you're going to send everybody on counselling courses and psychiatric care because they've heard a few guns go off, well you might as well not go to war, that's my opinion.

Not all survivors were picked up by their own side, as *Bill Mutimer*, Third Mate on the steamer SS *Harlesden*, discovered.

We were convinced by the time we got where we were that we were safe. We didn't expect a raider to intercept us there. In fact I was asleep at the time, when a plane started machine-gunning and bombing us. Without any sort of warning that I can remember, and it was some time before he dropped a message – whatever that said – so you might say it was a pretty unprovoked attack.

This was the first attack you'd faced?

Well, I'd been in convoys that were being attacked by U-boats, but we never copped it.

So you'd seen ships sunk around you?

Oh yes. You knew you were in the front line all right.

In fact the aircraft turned out to be the spotter plane from the German battle cruiser *Gneisenau*, making a sortie into the Atlantic in company with her sister ship *Scharnhorst* to disrupt British convoys. That night the unfortunate *Harlesden* was caught by the German battle group and sunk by shellfire, her crew taking to the lifeboats.

A light appeared fifty yards away well above our heads, and a guttural voice told us to come alongside. Ladders were hanging down, and I was shouting out for them not to touch my right arm as I went up. Then obviously I lay down and put my hand out for them to pick me up. They looked rather surprised, and then some chap sort of peered at me and asked me to follow him into a compartment that was lit up so he could see if I really was wounded. Being satisfied that I was he led me through the bowels of the ship. They looked after me as well as they possibly could – everything they could do for me they did. It wasn't good enough. I suppose penicillin would have been the answer in my case, but they did all they could.

He had to have his injured arm removed right to the shoulder, and was transferred from the *Gneisenau*, which had picked him up, to the supply ship *Ermland*.

Did you form an impression of what the Gneisenau *was like?*

When I did eventually get on deck it seemed a mighty battleship, with everything absolutely spic and span and efficient to every degree.

Did this worry you in relation to the war itself?

Well, only when I was lowered over the side of the ship and all round I saw the *Gneisenau*, I saw the *Scharnhorst*, I saw the two supply ships, and I thought my God! As I say, the Atlantic's an enormous place but all round you was the sight of German might, and you thought where's the bloody British Navy, it's non-existent.

On the supply ship the accent was on the showing what good chaps we are, and of course we're all sailors same as you and we might find ourselves in the same position. They were taking photographs of us on one occasion, one chap they jokingly called the Propaganda Minister, the doctor and somebody else, and we did say 'Why are you doing all this?' and the chap said 'We want to show the world that we're not Huns, we are decent fellows' [he shows me a copy of the German magazine in which the photos of himself appeared, to accompany an article extolling the excellent conditions enjoyed by British POWs]. We were taken to La Pallice, near La Rochelle, and just to emphasize that, that's me being lowered overboard [another photo]. When I got into the hospital it was just professionalism. Absolute professionalism. Particularly with this sister, Sister Elizabeth.

Did you realize that you would be a POW for some time to come?

Yes. Things were very bleak, there's no two ways about it, in those early days. Very bleak indeed. The fall of Crete. The sinking of the *Hood*. Greece being completely overrun. I heard all that, so I knew things were really bad.

I had three major operations and several sort of stitch-up and tidy-up jobs. I remember coming to after one operation and glancing down like that, and there was this thing bleeding. So I thought oh blow it! I can't face any more of this, so I just lay there. I suppose I would have been dead in a very short time, but then an orderly came up – 'Wie geht's Willem?' 'Oh, nicht gut' – and he lifted it up and immediately dashed away yelling for the doctor. And there I was out again choking! They placed this mask over your face and then sprayed chloroform on. Of course your legs are strapped, but you don't go out quietly like you would in a hospital nowadays, you go out struggling. I was really too weak to struggle, and that I suppose was what made it such a – well, such a terrible experience. The only thing that occurred to me when I thought I wouldn't survive was, well I shan't see what goes on – well, blow it. And that's all that I said to myself. I'd rather have lived just to see what happened, but I didn't think I wanted to go through all that pain and whatnot any longer. Yet as soon as I was getting better I certainly wanted to live, although things were again bad. Nearly every day you got these 'Sondermeldungs' as they called them, and everybody rushed down to the canteen and listened to the good news, from their point of view.

And you were picking up German by this time?

Yeah. It would have been very helpful if I'd had a dictionary, but it's amazing even now when I think about it, how much you pick up. Learning it the way I did, I hadn't got the least hesitation in speaking it regardless of whether my grammar was horrible or not.

Did your parents know you were safe?

The only news my parents had of me was by way of a short note which the hospital staff sent via Switzerland. Up till then they only had an official letter from the shipping company, J. & C. Harrison Ltd. [reads] 'It is with deep regret that we have to inform you that the above steamer is considerably overdue and we are advised by the Admiralty that she must be considered lost. Up to the present there is no news of either crew or steamer and we are afraid we can hold out very little hope of Mr Mortimer's (*sic*) survival but you may be assured we will immediately communicate with you if any news is received. We realize the great anxiety to which you are subjected by the absence of news and we take this opportunity of expressing our deepest sympathy.'

Eventually they sent me across France and into the Rhineland to a prison camp in North Germany.

What was that like?

Well, there was a time in early 1942 when no food parcels were coming through, I suppose it was still winter too, nothing coming off the farms, and it was grim – we were damned hungry. Then when the better weather came and the food parcels came along and we began to grow our own food we were reasonably – reasonably – well off. Probably could have done with a bit more, but I remember a fairly elderly American sea captain, he was still a rotund little chap, saying he'd lost a lot of weight and he'd never felt better in his life!

Were the prisoners well treated?

In general the Geneva Convention was observed, but I remember clearly a chap sitting in hospital with weals all over his back. I forget what he'd done, I think it was only some minor misdemeanour outside the camp, and they'd beaten him pretty badly. There was this Belgian chap they took out of the camp, and I saw them punch him before they took him away. Then there was the instance of the Russians pilfering our rations – the way they laid into them, if they fell they stayed there. What else was there? Oh, several chaps put in for different offences, into the bare prison cells they had there, just bread and water, and some of them had pretty bad bruises. But I didn't see a lot of it. I've got to be fair. Except when we first saw the Russians, that was absolutely ghastly. But so far as our people were concerned, the incidents were isolated.

Could you tell what was happening in Germany, outside the camp?

The only thing we did see – well not actually see – rather we heard for about three nights on end and sometimes during the day planes going over and the sound of gunfire. And for a week after that there was smoke and the smell of burning drifting across the camp. That was Hamburg – the firestorm raids.

What did you do to pass the time?

Oh, I filled my time studying maths and German, playing chess and helping in the parcels office. Or walking round the camp. It wasn't too bad.

And then we began to hear talk about repatriation, though it was in the air a long time before anything became firm.

After twenty months in German hands he was included in an exchange of prisoners, sailing across to neutral Sweden from Rostock, on the Baltic coast. On his return home he was taken to London for debriefing.

I remember on Waverley Station, Edinburgh, reporters coming up to us, but we were told not to communicate with the press until we'd been officially interviewed. I was interviewed up at the Admiralty in Whitehall by Holbrook, VC[6] and I gave him a full account of everything that had happened. And then it was a question of what would you like to drink, whisky or whatever. I asked him, 'What can I tell the press?' He said 'Tell them what you like. It doesn't matter now.'

And for others, like *Bill Smith*, being torpedoed was the start of an equal adventure.

We had to refuel at Aden, and while we were there I saw the *Repulse* and the *Prince of Wales* – they were just leaving. So we were in Aden for a couple of days, and we saw these big fellows go out, and we thought 'Oh well, if they're about it's got to be pretty safe', so we followed 'em down a couple of days later.

We'd got to two hundred miles south of Socotra Island when we were torpedoed by an enemy submarine. By this time we'd had enough rehearsals, it was a question of lifeboats and life-jackets, and grab your panic bag, and grab a reefer jacket; you've got time – she's going but she's not going that fast. You know you've got some time. What you're always really afraid of is that he'd be a bit impatient and let you have another one. Not forgetting the fact that we were in shark-infested waters so there was no leaping about into the water; we're into three lifeboats and away, standing off while she goes, which took a good twenty-five minutes. She made a hell of a noise. It was terrible to hear it.

And you sit there in the lifeboat and you think 'Christ, I've forgotten my watch'; or 'I've got my cigarettes but I haven't got any matches'; you think about all these things. And then it's all quiet for a while. But before we knew what was happening we got a searchlight on our boat and the sub's right beside us. We've got the First Officer with us – he's already collared the Captain from another lifeboat – so he took him on board; not

---

[6] Commander Norman Holbrook, who had won the VC as a submariner in the First World War

an easy thing to do at sea. Then through his loudspeaker he asked us the name of our ship and were we were going. I can't remember anything he said, there was quite a conversation; anyway, he took the Captain and the First Mate, and then he was gone. All of us were all ready to go over the side, sod it, sharks or not, if he got nasty with light machine guns or whatever. Anyway, he disappeared.

In the morning the sea was oily and calm, and for as far as you could see was debris. One of the terrible things about a ship sinking is that if your ship has gone down several miles and hit the bottom, and burst, anything which is buoyant like hatch covers or planks of wood would come to the surface like spears! They'd come staight out of the water! Would break your back or your leg, or kill you. A lot of rubbish comes rushing up to the surface as she goes down, which is quite frightening. Anyway, in the morning the sea was just an oily calm and as far as you could see was packing cases, bits of this, bits of that, everything floating. And in the middle of it all was his periscope.

The submarine stayed with them for five days, obviously hoping to pick off any vessel attracted by the lifeboats.

We had quite sophisticated lifesaving equipment – we had smoke flares; we had rockets; we had heliograph, which is mirrors; and we also had a radio transmitter which you had to crank up with your hands. The aerial was either held up in the sky with a small kite, or a balloon. And you'd keep cranking away, and they're tapping out, but of course by this time we'd drifted well away from where we were supposed to have been.

On the third day we saw this ship and we couldn't signal to him because of this bloody periscope! If we signalled to him he would come over and that would be the end of him! So there's sixty-four of us sitting in three lifeboats, and we let it go. The heart, the icy cold heart, it's as if your heart has got ice on it. He went. It was another couple of days before the periscope disappeared.

By this time we've got the masts up on all the lifeboats, and we've got a sail. And one of the lifeboats has got an engine. At

night we used to do a little bit of rowing, but not very enthusi-
astically because where are you going to row to? There was
nothing you could see.

We had oil lamps, so if you lit the oil lamp and hung it over
the side of the boat on a boathook the whole water would
boil with fish. All you had to do was strike out with the ship's
axe or anything else like that that was sharp, and you'd got all
the fish you wanted. Barracuda mostly. And with fish you get
fresh water – in the roe; if you cut a fish and you take the roe
out, the roe's got about an ounce of fresh water in it. You chew
it. It's like chewing a bedspread, but you've got fresh water. We
were in the lifeboats for more than three weeks. Our ration
consisted of an ounce of water – that's a spoonful – at five
o'clock in the morning. You got a boiled sweet, you got a
spoonful of some stuff like bacon fat, you had a biscuit which
was like a domino – might as well have been a domino because
you couldn't generate any saliva to eat it – two Horlicks milk
tablets like two aspirins – they were concentrated, so you used
to suck 'em; they used to last for hours – and then another
ounce of water when the sun went down. A little trick was to
cut a button off and suck that. By the time it was all over I
didn't have any buttons left – I'd swallowed them all! [laughs].
Another terrible thing is that under such circumstances you
don't go to the toilet – if you're not eating nothing's going
through you.

Big lifeboats, they go just as fast sideways as they do forwards, and we were saving the engine in case there was an
emergency and we did see a ship. Well on the twentieth day
there was a cloud on the horizon, but we were really more
worried about keeping out of the sun – nobody used to look
about too much. And the following day somebody said that's
the same cloud that was there yesterday. So when you start
really looking at it that's not a cloud, it's land! Now you've got
to get the three lifeboats together to discuss this; you can't do
anything without you all discuss it. 'Are you sure that was there
yesterday?' 'Yes, it's not moving – it's still there, you see.' So a
vote of confidence, yes we should go and have a look. We make
up lines, we start the engine, and we motor off towards it. This
is early in the morning, about six o'clock. Six o'clock at night

it's turning into something really definite – it's all right, we're making for land.

Well, it took an awfully long time to get there, and from hours out at sea you could see this land. It was Saudi Arabia. There was a large plain of brown arid land that went back about twenty miles straight up into brown mountains. There was nothing green about it at all. But it was solid. It was very interesting trying to land lifeboats in a surf that was about six foot high. We didn't have the strength or the energy to. Anyway, we all got ashore. The lifeboats got smashed up but we all got ashore. Sitting on the beach – at least it wasn't going up and down, it was all solid. Nothing in sight anywhere. There wasn't even a paper bag on the beach. We had a vague idea where we were, but we didn't really know. So we decided to march up the coast – if we stayed on the coast, sooner or later we'd be all right. That night we dug a big hole in the sand – it wasn't really sand, it was sort of like ash – and we all got in it, with the sails from the lifeboats pulled over us.

In the morning there was this terrible clatter, it was like people shaking dice in a cup. It was hermit crabs! It was like all the pebbles on Brighton beach on the move, and all coming clattering. Incredible. If you went near them they just disappeared.

We salvaged a few things from the lifeboats and set off down the coast. We saw an aeroplane about 30,000 feet high – he was just a tiny silver speck in the sky, you could just about see him, but no chance. Then a couple of hours later we saw one coming along the coast. He was about five miles out to sea, flying very low. So we set off our orange smoke flares, and at the same time with our hands we inscribed in the sand on the beach the name of the ship, the number of survivors, and a big arrow pointing the way in which we were going. He flew virtually out of sight before he turned round and came down the beach at about fifty feet, going like a bat out of hell. Of course, sixty-four blokes – he couldn't miss that. So he turned again, and as he came down and swooped over us he threw out a thermos flask – it was real Biggles – with a white scarf attached to it. Stay where you are, I'll report your position.

Fine. So we dug into the sand for another night, and in the

morning with the dawn, two Wellington bombers flew down the beach dropping supplies – tins of water, cigarettes, food, and lots of handkerchiefs which we were to pin on ourselves, about this size, in several dialects, saying to the Arabs that if they found us, British subjects, we would be ransomed by the British government if unharmed.

About three hours after that we were surrounded by the Bedouin. They just came from nowhere, obviously attracted by the aircraft. They were on horses, camels, on foot, armed to the teeth. They weren't hostile. They weren't over friendly, but they weren't hostile, so we went with them. That was about another two days' march down the coast, to a settlement – quite a big town. I remember further on there was a date plantation with dates. We were all put into a big courtyard – we weren't worried by this stage because everyone knew where we were – and we were given water, bread, and we ate that with the dates. Just to get a rest, not to be worried about anything was great.

And then two mornings later there was the sound of gunfire, and just off the coast was a big Navy destroyer. Ashore came the jolly boat with about ten sailors in it, with their tin hats, and their rifles. Negotiations were started, and I think we had to be paid for, but we all came back. We went out to the destroyer and were counted on board, very relieved to be back in civilization again. Taken to Aden, back where we started from. Into the hospital there, because we were all getting enormous – we were all becoming swollen. I couldn't do my trousers up – my top button wouldn't come within five inches of being done up. Still hadn't been to the toilet!

And then things began to go wrong. As soon as we were all in hospital, and all safe, then things started to go wrong. Our people started dying. I think it was probably shock, or it was the drama and the trauma of everything, it was too much, and quite a lot just gave up the ghost.

I was a couple of weeks in hospital; everything started working again. We were taken down the town in batches of five, given a great big suitcase and a white linen suit, canvas shoes, a panama hat, couple of cotton shirts, some cotton singlets, some handkerchiefs and the rest of it. I looked like something out of a cheap movie! In a couple of days we were put on a troopship to Port Said, then on up to Suez, then home.

We buried two more of our crew on the way home. Funerals at sea. They just gave up, that's the best way that I can describe it. It's not that he's bleeding or coughing, he just sits down and dies. Or just doesn't wake up in the morning. So that was the last piece of my wartime action. When the war eventually ended I just couldn't stop crying.

I just cried and cried all the time, that it was all over.